LITTLE BOOK OF
SOCIOLOGY

Rasha Barrage

summersdale

THE LITTLE BOOK OF SOCIOLOGY

Crowd icon © galaira/Shutterstock.com

An Hachette UK Company
www.hachette.co.uk

Summersdale Publishers Ltd
Part of Octopus Publishing Group Limited
Carmelite House
50 Victoria Embankment
LONDON
EC4Y 0DZ
UK

www.summersdale.com

Printed and bound in the China

ISBN: 978-1-80007-718-8

Contents

Introduction

Societies, unlike individuals, are not clearly defined. There are no precise names or physical outlines, and their structures and principles are ever-changing. Yet the power of society to shape a person's life can be profound. Take your decision to read this book; perhaps you selected a "little" book because you are time-poor, or your curiosity about sociology was not fulfilled at school. You may not realize it, but there might be wider reasons influencing your choice that only a sociologist can detect. These could be a number of different reasons – political policies regarding education, the structure of the working week, living costs or the way the publishing industry has evolved. Tensions between personal autonomy and the influence of society over individual choice lie at the heart of sociology. Therefore, delving into this discipline can alter how you view your life and the world around you. By introducing you to the key sociological ideas, this book reveals the subtle forces that might be patterning your own behaviour, from everyday decisions to your relationships and career. You will also see the role sociology can play in solving global problems.

WHAT IS
SOCIOLOGY?

The term "sociology" is a combination of the Latin "*socius*", meaning companion or associate, and the Greek "*logiā*" meaning the study of. Today, sociology can be summarized as the systematic (or organized) study of human societies. But such a definition fails to grasp the discipline's huge breadth and possibilities. Sociology examines countless dimensions of human social interaction, from the experiences of individuals and social groupings to the largest institutions and organizations of a society. It is concerned with the patterns, conditions, interactions and processes affecting billions of people worldwide; its potential scope is as large as its subject matter and continues to similarly evolve. This chapter introduces some of the different perspectives used by sociologists in grappling with this immense subject. You will discover the most popular research methods as well as the ethical issues that often arise for sociologists when conducting their work. With a clearer understanding of what sociology is, you will see how it can inspire social change and permanently transform your perspective.

The "psychology of society"

The term **"social science"** refers to the branches of science that are concerned with the study of societies and social relationships, namely: anthropology, economics, political science, psychology and sociology. There is a lot of overlap between these disciplines; for instance, both psychology and sociology involve the scientific study of human thought processes and behaviours and seek to improve people's lives, and anthropology looks at how societies and cultures develop. What distinguishes sociology is its focus on social groups, communities and cultures – it looks beyond individuals by taking a bird's eye view of social dynamics, patterns and trends. Sociology looks at society at all levels and all scales, from family structures to globalization.

A DIFFERENT PERSPECTIVE

The sociologist Kai T. Erikson has said that sociology is "a perspective rather than a body of knowledge", and that sociologists are distinguished from other social observers, such as historians or economists, not by "*what* we see but the *way* we see".

Big and small questions

Sociologists study society by adopting one of the following levels of approach:

MACRO-LEVEL SOCIOLOGY

- Focuses on wider social systems and structures.
- Studies large-scale groups, institutions or populations.
- Asks big questions such as: In what ways has class shaped the development of society? To what extent does ethnicity affect our opportunities in life? How will the climate crisis alter relationships between nations?

MICRO-LEVEL SOCIOLOGY

- Focuses on small-scale human relations, typically at the community level, but can also include interactions between couples or friends.
- Studies everyday face-to-face interactions and group scenarios.
- Asks more focused, narrow questions, like: How do working parents balance their roles and identities? Do police officers approach people differently according to their age?

The macro and micro-level approaches complement each other. Just as the natural world is understood through a combination of biology, physics and chemistry, a comprehensive picture of the social world encompasses both large-scale arrangements of a society and the behaviour of its individual members. Both are significant and constantly influencing each other. The two perspectives allow sociologists to gain a greater understanding of humanity and how large-scale patterns and trends influence the behaviour and experiences of individuals and groups, and vice versa.

MICRO-SOCIOLOGY

Georges Gurvitch argued that there are levels to social reality and coined the term "micro-sociology" in 1939 (borrowing the expression from microphysics). Unlike the large-scale studies of social psychology, sociology and social anthropology, micro-sociology focused on specific interpersonal interactions between individuals and groups.

How do sociologists work?

The research methods adopted by sociologists fall into two broad categories: **quantitative** and **qualitative**. Both aim to interpret patterns and relationships in society, but the big divide between the two is the kinds of data they use.

Researchers who collect **quantitative data** apply statistical analysis techniques to relatively large data sets of people. This data can be presented in numerical form, such as surveys asking people closed questions which can then be turned into numbered responses and analyzed, or it might involve administrative data collected by institutions (e.g. data collected on crime or schools). Quantitative methods include:

- Lab and field experiments
- Structured interviews or observations
- Questionnaires (paper or online) featuring either closed questions or those that have a finite number of responses
- Opinion polls and surveys presentable in charts or diagrams, such as voting intentions
- Official statistics, such as exam results

Researchers who collect **qualitative data** tend to use long interviews with a small number of people, drawing conclusions from analyzing what people say. This data is presented in written or visual formats. For instance, a sociologist could undertake participant observation by observing people doing a particular job and deriving insights from their speech and behaviour. Qualitative methods include:

- Questionnaires featuring open questions
- Surveys conducted online, door-to-door, by phone or mail
- Field research including unstructured interviews, participant observations (covert or overt) and focus groups so broader ranges of responses can be analyzed
- Case studies involving in-depth research into individuals or groups
- Sociometric tests measuring interpersonal relations
- Secondary sources that are not produced with the intention of being analyzed, such as medical histories
- Content analysis, such as researching books or photography

Ethical issues

There are many potential ethical issues that sociologists must consider when planning and conducting their research. There are established **ethical guidelines** (or written codes of conduct), which set the standards of practice and what is considered acceptable. If these guidelines are breached, researchers can encounter ethical problems regarding participants' consent, anonymity or confidentiality. For instance, research involving data gathered from online fora or discussion platforms can generate concerns about the informed consent, privacy and anonymity of the human participants. Some have likened data research to a form of "electronic eavesdropping". Contacting potential participants can also be viewed as "spamming", which is itself an invasion of privacy.

APPROACHES TO RESEARCH

Inductive research ("bottom-up approach") involves searching for patterns from a set of observations and generating a theory from the data obtained. Often associated with qualitative research, this approach is taken when sociologists know little about the social issue at hand.

The masses of personal and impersonal data (known as **big data**) available in society, and the tools to analyze them, pose moral dilemmas. Study participants should give informed consent (understand what the research is about and what taking part involves), but researchers can access swathes of potentially sensitive data without engaging with participants. Large data sets coupled with complex algorithms have caused new kinds of injury, from legal or psychological harm to informational harm, such as algorithmic discrimination (e.g. racial or gender bias) or privacy breaches.

CHALLENGING SOCIAL ETHICS

All societies have assumptions about what is morally acceptable behaviour, and sociologists critically analyze these values. For example, Laurie and Matthew Taylor's 2003 book *What Are Children For?* used data from various countries to explore the conflict between individualism and the demands of child-rearing.

What is society?

Sociology can be defined in many ways, but one common feature is the notion of **society**. A society is a group of people who share a geographic location and who enter various relationships with each other. These relationships are governed by the rules, regulations, norms and values of the location, which are constantly changing and therefore provide a vast resource for sociological research.

One of the founders of sociology, Auguste Comte, viewed society as a collective organism similar to a human body; with forms of social power being "the tissue", family providing the "elements" and cities behaving as "organs". He believed the parts of the body (individuals) could only be understood through knowledge of the whole (society).

IS "SOCIETY" STILL RELEVANT?

Since the 1970s, sociologists have debated whether sociology should shift its focus away from societies. Scholars such as Alain Touraine have concentrated on individuals and their interactions, while others like John Urry suggest that globalization has resulted in "global networks and flows" replacing societies.

Questioning society

In many ways, sociology can be seen as the ultimate theoretical rebellion. Rather than simply accepting or bemoaning the way a society is organized, sociologists identify and challenge its conventional truths and norms. Thinking like a sociologist means you ask fundamental questions, like: Why is this acceptable? How does this behaviour impact others? What are the subtle influences? Sociologists attempt to investigate such questions objectively, putting aside their personal opinions in the hope of understanding fundamental causes and consequences. For instance, capitalism dominates much of the world in the twenty-first century, and while its existence may appear necessary (and desirable) for society to function effectively, is it the only possible social system? For many sociologists, their work goes beyond analysis and description; their research is used to address inequalities in society and potentially alter people's attitudes to existing social practices. Their findings can also inform public policy and be a driver for social change.

A BRIEF
HISTORY OF
SOCIOLOGY

Across the centuries and around the world, people have been curious about how society works. Many historians, philosophers, religious leaders and writers have attempted to describe and compare different societies. As a result, there is no single approved history of sociology or sociological thinking. However, the scientific discipline of sociology is commonly believed to have begun in the nineteenth century by a few individuals in Europe. So, why has the label of "sociologist" been assigned to these figures but not their predecessors? What caused the field of sociology to be created 200 years ago, and how has it evolved since then? In answering these questions, this chapter reveals the pioneering ideas of key people, together with the main intellectual trends and schools of thought that have dominated the field. As the search for an ideal society remains as elusive and fascinating as ever, you will see how many ideas and themes that shaped sociology's origin continue to be relevant today.

Timeline of early sociological thought

TIME	EVENT
484–425 BCE	The Greek historian Herodotus writes *Histories*, which describes variations in the norms of societies around the Mediterranean.
484–425 BCE	The Greek philosopher Plato considers society as a unified system and explores how a society should be organized.
384–322 BCE	Aristotle attempts to classify social systems such as governments, and questions what makes a just society.
Thirteenth century CE	The Chinese historian Ma Tuan-Lin explores how social dynamics shape historical developments.
Fourteenth century	The Tunisian historian Ibn Khaldun analyzes "the nature of things which are born of civilization", comparing nomadic and sedentary lifestyles and how social cohesion impacts power. Some consider him to be the world's first sociologist.

TIME	EVENT
Sixteenth/ seventeenth centuries	Thomas Hobbes (1588–1679) argues that social bonds and the state provide social order and harmony. John Locke (1632–1704) writes that social inequality and conflict arise because of private property.
Early eighteenth century	Jean-Jacques Rousseau (1712–78) argues that society creates more complex needs for humanity. The French philosopher Baron de Montesquieu's book *The Spirit of Laws* (1748) examines different institutions and formulates the principle of a separation of powers.
Late eighteenth century	Edinburgh was the "Athens of the North"; intellectuals including Adam Smith (1723–90), Adam Ferguson (1723–1816), John Millar (1735–1801) and William Robertson (1721–93) believe society is born out of human nature and is created through structure and process.
1813	Henri de Saint-Simon (1760–1825) proposes a science of society and introduces the concept of an "industrial society".

TIME	EVENT
1838	Auguste Comte (1798–1857) uses the term "sociology" to describe a new social science (word first used in 1780 by Emmanuel-Joseph Sieyès (1748–1836).
1848	Karl Marx (1818–1883) and Friedrich Engels (1820–1895) co-author *The Communist Manifesto*, which includes arguments about the inequalities of capitalism and the division of social classes.
1890s	First departments of sociology established at the University of Bordeaux and the University of Chicago. Émile Durkheim's (1858–1917) work focuses on the division of labour and mechanical versus organic solidarity. His pioneering study on suicide published 1897.
Start of twentieth century	Sociology established as a distinct discipline of study. By 1910, most universities across Europe and the USA are offering sociology courses.

A new discipline

Known as the "Father of Sociology", Frenchman Auguste Comte defined the term "sociology" in 1838 to describe a new science of society. Influenced by Henri de Saint-Simon, Comte argued that the social world could be studied using the same principles as the natural sciences, and that this approach would reveal the "laws" governing our social lives. He believed that knowledge of these scientific "facts" would enable sociologists to effect social change for a more positive future.

BUT IS IT A SCIENCE?

Proponents of the scientific study of social patterns, such as Auguste Comte and Émile Durkheim, are known as **positivists**. They believe scientific research methods can identify natural/universal laws and patterns of human behaviour that enable us to understand society's functions.

Antipositivists, like Max Weber and Karl Popper, have argued that, while sociology can only be regarded as a science when it is methodical in its use of scientific techniques, at the same time, absolute truths are not attainable; universal laws of behaviour do not always apply.

Origins of sociology

Sociological thinking has roots stretching back to ancient times. For centuries, writing by numerous philosophers and historians had been going beyond the mere description of historical facts. Plato, Ma Tuan-Lin and Ibn Khaldun are some of the most famous intellectuals to have proposed theories about cultural comparisons, how societies function, why conflict occurs and the causes of social change, but their work was not labelled or conceptualized in the way that sociology is today. The term that is commonly used for these earliest efforts is **"proto-sociology"**, as they contain the essential ingredients of sociology but the word and the discipline did not exist at the time of their publication.

THE INFLUENCE OF LANGUAGE

The Ancient Greeks distinguished between *physis* (nature, without human intervention) and *nomos* (laws or customs that restrict human behaviour), a distinction which some view as the foundation of sociology. The sociological term **"norm"**, meaning a social rule that guides your behaviour, originates from *nomos*.

The modern discipline of sociology emerged during the eighteenth century; a time of unprecedented change.

- **The "Enlightenment"** – an intellectual revolution whereby scientific discoveries and technological advancements challenged the dominance of religious belief and explanation.

- **The Industrial Revolution** – the shift from agriculture and village living to factories and city dwelling transformed the way society was organized and how people worked. The emergence of capitalism established new socioeconomic classes.

- **The French Revolution of 1789–99** – a period of major social upheaval in France that saw the overthrow of the monarchy.

Enlightenment philosophers questioned why these events were happening and how society could improve. For instance, if kings were not ordained by an almighty power, how could anyone justify their rule, and who should govern instead? One philosopher saw the need for a rational and scientific understanding of social processes. His name was Auguste Comte.

Émile Durkheim

A founding father of the discipline, French philosopher Émile Durkheim believed that sociologists should study objective "social facts". These are realities external to, and that exert control over, the individual. Examples today might be a country's legal system, its class structure or population distribution. By conducting studies beyond the context of individual actions, Durkheim believed that societies could be diagnosed as either "healthy" or "pathological".

SOLIDARITY

Ibn Khaldun wrote that "*asabiyyah*", meaning group feeling or a sense of shared purpose, is central to the survival of a society. He viewed it as the basic motivational force of history. Durkheim similarly argued that beliefs hold a society together and the health of a society can only be maintained through "solidarity". He distinguished between traditional "mechanical solidarity", where there is a sense of community, shared beliefs and what he called "collective consciousness", versus "organic solidarity" where relationships are formed through shared specializations and interdependence.

Religion and social impact

Durkheim questioned why industrialization and the rise of capitalism was causing greater unhappiness. His 1897 work, *Suicide*, asserted that suicide had social causes. After analyzing statistics across nations and social groups, Durkheim identified a correlation between higher suicide rates and Protestantism. Unlike Catholic societies, where community, consolation and a "collective consciousness" were paramount, Protestant communities were characterized by individualism, and "failure" was attributed directly to a person's behaviour. Family ties and the social institutions provided by long-established faiths were disintegrating and being replaced with a new emphasis on individualism. Durkheim argued that industrialization, emerging from Protestant values, caused people to feel disconnected, devoid of purpose and more vulnerable to suicide.

ANOMIE (NORMLESSNESS)

The sociological term **"anomie"** was introduced by Durkheim to describe an unstable social condition whereby previously dominant values disappear and no new values develop in their place.

Functionalism

Durkheim was also instrumental in developing sociology's first major theoretical approach; functionalism. This theory asserts that all aspects of a society serve a function; just as a human body is composed of interrelated and interdependent parts, society has a similar structure. The focus is on what maintains a society, not what changes it. Durkheim viewed society as a system, with each part (norms, customs, traditions and institutions) playing a necessary role. For instance, religion and the economy are organs while individuals are the cells within these organisms. The parts work together to maintain social order, consensus and stability.

SOCIAL EQUILIBRIUM

In sociology, the term "**social**" or "**dynamic equilibrium**" applies to a stable society where all the components are working well together. For the sociologist Talcott Parsons, learning to socialize and exercise self-control are the key processes that allow a society to achieve this balance.

Society is not a mere sum of individuals. Rather, the system formed by their association represents a specific reality which has its own characteristics.
Émile Durkheim

The social anthropologist A. R. Radcliffe-Brown developed this idea further by introducing the theory of **structural functionalism**. Inspired by the work of Auguste Comte, he argued that society was a separate level of reality distinct from individuals. For Radcliffe-Brown and many sociologists of the early twentieth century, social structures contributed to the function of society as a whole.

Functionalism was revived in the USA during the 1950s and 1960s by Talcott Parsons and Robert K. Merton. Merton distinguished between **manifest** (intended or overtly recognized) functions and **latent** (unintended or unrecognized) functions of social institutions. For instance, a manifest function of school is the transmission of knowledge, while a latent function is socialization.

The functionalist perspective declined from the 1970s, due to critics highlighting its failure to explain social change or the existence of dysfunction and the way it ignored individuals within a society.

Marxism and conflict theory

You may be familiar with the German philosopher and economist Karl Marx as a socialist thinker. What he is perhaps less well known for are the numerous concepts about society that he devised, and which remain hugely influential to sociology.

Unlike Comte's positivism which was based on the pursuit of social harmony and stability, Marx viewed conflict as the central cause of social change. He formulated the concept of **social class** (rather than groups, castes or elites) to explain the division of labour brought about by the industrial revolution. For Marx, capitalist society was characterized by a conflict between two primary classes: the minority, dominant rulers and factory owners (bourgeoisie/ruling class) who controlled the means of production, versus the majority, labourers and factory workers (proletariat/working class) who owned little and remained poor due to **exploitation**. He thereby introduced the idea of **class conflict**. This meant that the basis of power had shifted to the ownership of capital rather than land, as had been the case in the previous mode of production; feudalism.

Marx argued that this new social division created **alienation** for the working class, who were alienated from the products of their own labour, dehumanized by their work and estranged from their "species-essence" (human nature). The working class would eventually become aware of their oppression (by gaining what he called "**class consciousness**") and organize revolutionary action to build a fairer society. Though Marx's prediction of a communist revolution did not occur across industrialized nations, several revolutions in the twentieth century based on his ideas happened in semi-industrialized or agrarian non-Western societies such as Russia and China. In the West, his scientific studies of society continue to be explored by sociologists today.

HISTORICAL MATERIALISM

Marx and Engels presented a new theory of historical progress called **historical materialism** which claimed that society is organized and changes according to the material conditions in which people live. So, the transition from feudalism to capitalism in Europe occurred because of new methods in economic production (from agricultural land to machinery in factories).

Max Weber

The German sociologist Max Weber (1864–1920) adopted many aspects of Marx's conflict theory. However, while Marx focused his theories on the economic changes of the nineteenth century, Weber believed that the major transformation and driving force behind capitalism, and any form of social change, is ideological.

Writing during the time of the industrial revolution, Weber believed that the changes he witnessed were (unintentionally) brought about by the spread of Protestant ideas – in particular, Calvinism. For this reason, Weber argued that objective scientific methods were not enough for the study of society or to predict social behaviour. He believed researchers themselves were incapable of putting aside their own cultural and moral biases and that culture was critical to human behaviour. In seeking an alternative approach, Weber introduced the concept of *verstehen* (pronounced *fair-shtay-en* and loosely means "understanding"), which explores the interaction between individuals and cultures by requiring the researchers to put themselves in the position of the people being studied.

Rationalization was another radical concept of Weber's. He noted that capitalism required rational decision-making where the only goal was economic gain. With this came a sense of "disenchantment" and a rise in bureaucracy. The increase in factories and large-scale workforces meant that efficiency, standardized procedures, personal discipline and rigid regulations became paramount. Religious constraints were replaced with new forms of control that similarly stifled people's individualism. Weber likened the modern era to an "iron cage" that threatened freedom and trapped us all.

Symbolic interactionism

The twentieth century saw sociology expand into the USA. This brought a shift in focus from institutions or structures to micro-level interactions between individuals or small groups. The American philosopher George Herbert Mead believed that self-image was formed through social interactions and language. From the 1960s, ideas about how people understand society through communication began to be tested further. Mead's student, Herbert Blumer, coined the term **"symbolic interactionism"** to describe this approach.

This theory focuses on how things work in day-to-day life. Proponents believe that individuals are not passive bystanders but are active participants in the social world through their interpretation of objects, people and situations. This means our view of society, institutions and the actions of others are treated as symbolic forms that influence our behaviour. Who we are and how we perceive ourselves is defined by our social interactions and the institutions we encounter. Society then is not a structure (as the functionalists argued) but a continual process, formed through the meanings that people attach to social interactions.

Status and role

Symbolic interactionism pivots on the concepts of social status and "self". In 1936, the anthropologist Ralph Linton distinguished between status and role:

- 👤 **Status** is a socially defined position, such as student or father. This forms part of your identity, how you relate to others and confers rights and obligations. It can be **ascribed** (assigned at birth or involuntarily, such as sex, age or citizenship) or **achieved** (acquired through effort, such as becoming a teacher or doctor). All the statuses you hold create your **status set**, and the one that you are most associated with is your **master status.**

- 👤 **Role** refers to the behaviour that is expected of a person with a particular status or social position. A single status may have many roles within it, called a **role set**. For instance, the role of a teacher is comprised of relationships with a school, students, parents and colleagues.

- 👤 You may experience **role conflict** if you occupy contradictory roles (e.g. student and employee), or **role strain** if it overwhelms you.

Impression management

Long before the emergence of social media, sociologists were exploring ideas about how we present ourselves to others and interpret reactions to the image we present. According to sociologist Charles Horton Cooley, we "live in the minds of others without knowing it", meaning that we develop an idea of ourselves based on how we are perceived by others – what he called "**the looking-glass self**". Social interaction serves as a mirror, and our values, behaviour and self-worth are formed through the judgement of others.

Erving Goffman was fascinated with impression management and how we act and behave around others; what he termed the "**interaction order**". He argued that people present images of themselves depending on what is expected of them by society in any given situation. Wider social structures can therefore be understood through observing interactions, including the unspoken customs and rules of behaviour that shape these exchanges. To Goffman, even the activity of speaking was a social, rather than a linguistic, construct.

FIGURATION

Norbert Elias coined the term **"figuration"** to describe the interdependence of individuals and society. Just like the players in a team sport, the structure and dynamics of figurations are constantly changing and serve to both limit and enable individual action.

Goffman viewed people as actors on a social stage, each with a unique role to play and cultural "scripts" to follow. Every interaction requires a person to project an identity that guides the behaviour of others – what he referred to as "virtual" (front stage) or "actual" (back stage) social identity. Virtual identity refers to our public, socially legitimate persona whereas actual identity means the personality we possess in private. Rather than possessing a fixed self, he believed that the self was a social process.

Arlie R. Hochschild developed these ideas by considering the emotional management required by some professions, for example, flight attendants or cashiers being expected to always be friendly and smile. She called this ability to suppress and produce feelings **"emotional labour"**.

Sociological imagination

Neither the life of an individual nor the history of a society can be understood without understanding both.
C. Wright Mills

The American sociologist C. Wright Mills coined the term **"sociological imagination"** to describe the sociological way of thinking. Put simply, this is a mindset that allows you to connect personal matters to wider social issues. For Mills, the study of society is only effective if sociological imagination is applied. He believed this ability was critical to understanding the relationship between individuals and systems and identifying the structural cause of problems that are shared by millions of people (such as divorce, drug addiction, loneliness or poverty).

Mills argued that sociologists must look beyond the individual person and their situation in life ("biography") to the broader picture of influence ("history"), including a person's race, class, gender and the history and culture of their location which all intersect to shape values, character and behaviour.

Sociological imagination allows you to recognize private "troubles" as public "issues" and see the sociological reality of your existence and the existence of others. For instance, in considering an unemployed individual, sociological imagination lets you see beyond the person's personal circumstances, psychology or insecurities to the wider context, such as the state of the economy, government policies or the skills that are in demand. Likewise, a student at a top university may be intelligent but their admission was also impacted by family background, access to financing and early education opportunities in their country.

SOCIAL JUSTICE

Mills believed that identifying a person's place in the bigger picture of history allows sociologists to expose social injustice and take action to improve society. In this way, sociology has a moral and political role. This critical and "countersystem" approach can be seen in the work of Harriet Martineau or W. E. B. Du Bois. But not everyone agrees with this approach to sociology; many scholars since the 1940s have focused on discovering knowledge about society rather than presenting arguments for improving it.

Feminism

Feminism, meaning support for the equality of genders, is often associated with activism. But in sociological terms, it is a distinct school of thought within the study of gender. The perspective developed through three phases:

First wave feminism (nineteenth to early twentieth century) – the start of the women's rights movement, which dealt with the right to vote and property rights.

Second wave feminism (1960s-80s) – referred to as "women's liberation", this phase focused on anti-discrimination, equal pay, reproductive rights and equality. The idea that gender has societal origins started to spread through books like *The Feminine Mystique* (1963) by Betty Friedan.

Third wave feminism (1990s-2000s) – a backlash to the second wave's focus on issues most relevant to white, heterosexual or middle-class women. The definition of feminism broadened to capture other forms of discrimination such as race or class.

...to be "feminist" in any authentic sense of the term is to want for all people, female and male, liberation from sexist role patterns, domination and oppression.

bell hooks

Ain't I a Woman: Black Women and Feminism, 1981

PATRIARCHY: A CULTURAL CONSTRUCT

Patriarchy, a word derived from Ancient Greek meaning "rule of the father", is the opposite of feminism and refers to a society in which privileged and dominant positions are held by men. The historian Gerda Lerner traced its roots to Mesopotamia around 5,000 years ago, during the transition from subsistence living to agriculture.

The story of feminism began long before the "first wave". Christine de Pizan was defending the role of women in the fifteenth century through her writings on women's equality, and several "proto-feminist" works exist such as Marie de Gournay's *The Equality of Men and Women* published in 1622, and Mary Wollstonecraft's *A Vindication of the Rights of Woman* in 1792. However, the surge in feminist activity in the late nineteenth century was unparalleled and took inspiration from the Abolitionist Movement in the US.

Sociology of race

The American sociologist W. E. B. Du Bois wrote a pioneering essay collection in 1903 titled *The Souls of Black Folk*, which famously said that "the problem of the twentieth century is the problem of the colour-line". Through his studies of communities within the southern states of the US, he exposed the racism embedded within the economic and social structures of society. He noted that respect, opportunities and power were only given to white people, and Black people remained "slaves of society". Applying a rigorous use of empirical data and interviews, he was the first sociologist to move beyond observation to detailed investigative research of actual living and working conditions – a cornerstone of race studies today.

"DOUBLE CONSCIOUSNESS"

Du Bois argued that African Americans integrating into American society were forced to always see themselves through the eyes of others. The awareness of being both American (valuing equality and fairness) and Black (subject to contempt and denied opportunities) caused a fractured identity where "one ever feels his twoness".

Race-conflict theory

Du Bois was perhaps the first sociologist to apply conflict theory to race. He observed that a racially divided society served the interests of economic and political elites. Racism prevented the development of a politically united class of labourers (both Black and white), which allowed their exploitation to continue unchallenged.

> *The cause of freedom is not the cause of a race or a sect, a party or a class — it is the cause of humankind, the very birthright of humanity.*
> **Anna J. Cooper**

In 1892, Anna J. Cooper, the "mother of Black feminism", wrote *A Voice from the South*, where she examined multiple perspectives and overlapping struggles (what we now call "**intersectionality**"). In observing social conflict, she argued that all standpoints should be heard, including that of the Black woman. Her assertion that race, class *and* gender were worthy of attention was ground-breaking and contested dominant ideas. Long before C. Wright Mills, she held the belief that sociologists could further social justice.

Contemporary sociology

Sociological thinking changed in the mid-twentieth century. Moving on from structural-functionalist perspectives and systematic grand theories, a new generation of sociologists began to explore a vast array of topics. The changing geopolitical landscape also created new areas of focus, such as multiculturalism and globalization (see chapter three). Questions about why a society is structured in a particular way or how individuals interact continued to be asked, but the range of possible answers transformed and multiplied. Every aspect of society, and even our understanding of "reality", was to be turned on its head and examined.

A YOUNG SCIENCE

Thomas Kuhn's *The Structure of Scientific Revolutions* (1962) explained how development in any scientific field happens through phases of **shifting paradigms** (common intellectual frameworks or fundamentals). He argued that sociology was not a mature science because there was no shared set of assumptions about society or how it should be researched; there was no **unifying paradigm**.

Knowledge as power

French philosopher Michel Foucault had a strong influence on contemporary sociology. He believed that power was present at every level of society. Rather than a simple system of oppression, power is enacted via a web of social expectations and assumptions. Foucault adopted the term **"discourse"** to describe a form of communication that is controlled and limited by social filters and taboos which then define the norms of social reality. Even "truth" depends on what is authorized by the dominant discourse. He coined the term **"power-knowledge"** to describe how power is exercised through controlling the acceptable forms of knowledge and excluding others.

SURVEILLANCE AND CONTROL

The English philosopher Jeremy Bentham developed the concept of the **"panopticon"** to describe how an individual prison guard can monitor multiple prisoners, and how this threat of observation serves as a constant means of control. Foucault extended this argument by claiming that we all internalize power relationships to self-regulate our behaviour.

Constructing reality

Late twentieth-century sociology was preoccupied with the influence of culture on human behaviour. One theory that falls within this long tradition is **social constructivism** (or social constructionism), which claims that all aspects of social life and identity, and therefore your perception of reality, are constructed. Peter L. Berger and Thomas Luckmann's book *The Social Construction of Reality* (1966) argued that "reality" is not an objective truth but is constructed through a kind of social consensus. So, what seems "natural" or "obvious" to you is an invention of a particular culture and may not necessarily merit the same meaning or consequence in another culture. Michel Foucault is a key advocate of this theory; for instance, he noted that people experiencing "madness" were once viewed as possessing a kind of "wisdom" and were revered in some circles, but from the seventeenth century they were subject to increasing medical interventions and institutionalization. Instead of being treated with respect or curiosity, madness became an illness that needed to be "cured".

Individual action

Pay to the most commonplace activities of daily life the attention usually accorded extraordinary events.
Harold Garfinkel

The sociologist Harold Garfinkel developed Talcott Parsons' idea of examining the roots of social order rather than its "rules". He believed that rules and social structures arose out of the everyday interactions of individuals, so it is these small exchanges that should be the focus of study. He called this "bottom up" rather than "top down" approach **ethnomethodology**.

In the 1980s, Anthony Giddens incorporated Garfinkel's ideas in his **structuration theory** which proposed that every social encounter reproduces or transforms society. So, every time you interact with others, you are acting as an agent of change or an active creator of society. Though he claimed that the scope of change is bound by the resources and practices of history, it is the continuity of the past and the reproduction in the present (by individual actors) which brings about structuration. Social change therefore comes about when large numbers of people break social patterns and create movements.

MAJOR
TOPICS IN
SOCIOLOGY

An ongoing and central debate within sociology concerns structure versus agency. This can be likened to the nature versus nurture debate in biology, as it questions how much of your life (or your ability to act independently) has been determined by pre-existing social arrangements that have shaped and constrained your behaviour. In exploring this question, sociologists have studied a huge number of topics, and new subjects are constantly being introduced in response to changes in social structures and global events. For instance, in 2022 the American Sociological Association (ASA) had 53 sections of study, including the Sociology of Indigenous Peoples and Native Nations announced in 2020. This chapter introduces you to some of the responses to the question of structure versus agency, and the major themes that have occupied sociologists for over 100 years, from class and social stratification to issues concerning crime, education and gender. As you read on, your sociological imagination will be revealed to you as you discover a variety of social forces that intersect and shape who you are today.

Three approaches

Before diving into some of the major topics of sociology, it is worth understanding the different assumptions guiding researchers when they approach a subject. Sociological studies usually adopt one of the following three major theoretical perspectives which you were introduced to in chapter two:

PERSPECTIVE	LEVEL OF ANALYSIS	VIEW OF SOCIETY
Functionalist	Macro	Stability within society is maintained through different parts of society operating together to keep it moving (e.g. Durkheim and Comte).
Conflict	Macro	Society is unequal and defined by struggle. Social structures benefit some people at the expense of others (e.g. Marx).
Symbolic interaction	Micro	Individuals create society through their interactions (e.g. George Herbert Mead).

There are also meso-, or mid-range, theories which focus on social institutions, companies or organizations.

Social stratification

Social stratification refers to the hierarchical arrangement of large social groups based on categories such as class, race, gender, age and other attributes that are valued by society. It basically refers to inequality; an issue that has been the focus of attention for many sociologists. It must be considered within every area of study because stratification is universal across all societies, though it comes in a variety of forms.

While you might have always assumed that social classifications are a matter of individual differences and choices (such as occupation or geographic location), stratification is in fact a characteristic of society. The way a society arranges itself into groups impacts people's life chances regardless of their individual traits. For instance, children born into poverty are often more likely to have a shorter life span and spend less time in education than their wealthier counterparts. Social stratification has a huge impact on your life, from the type of education you have, to your occupation and access to healthcare.

Social mobility

Social mobility refers to changes in position within the social hierarchy. **Horizontal mobility** means changing your role while maintaining the same position in the hierarchy, such as starting a new job that provides a similar wage and social status. **Vertical mobility** is an upward or downward movement within the hierarchy, such as a student from a low-income background graduating from medical school and becoming a doctor. The option to move "levels" depends on whether it is a closed or open stratification system:

- Closed systems allow little to no mobility through legal restrictions and formally defined categories. Your position is **ascribed** (determined at birth or assumed involuntarily later in life). The caste system in India is an example of this.

- Open systems allow mobility between categories that are often blurred. Your status is usually **achieved** through personal accomplishments. Class-based societies are an example of this, such as the USA (though barriers to mobility remain, as the rest of this chapter explains).

Societal or public policy changes can also bring about **structural social mobility** by forcing large-scale movements of people within the hierarchy. Examples include the decline in so-called "blue collar" jobs (manufacturing or manual labour) since the early twentieth century, and the rise in "white collar" occupations (clerical or managerial duties). Sociologists have highlighted the importance of social mobility for class formation and structure. For instance, Anthony Giddens argued that low rates of social mobility cause higher rates of class solidarity among individuals (feelings of shared affinity and interests between members of the same class).

"I SHOP, THEREFORE I AM"

In 1899, the symbolic interactionist Thorstein Veblen coined the phrase **"conspicuous consumption"** to describe the way people buy lavish or impractical items to attain or maintain a given social status (such as branded clothing, expensive cars or mansions). At its most extreme, people engage in **"invidious consumption"** to purposely make others jealous, or **"conspicuous compassion"**, which is charitable giving to boost your reputation and social prestige.

Why is society unequal?

The answer depends on your sociological perspective:

- Functionalists, such as Kingsley Davis and Wilbert Moore, argue that the unequal distribution of rewards is necessary and inevitable. The **Davis-Moore thesis** of 1945 concluded that jobs with the greatest responsibility for maintaining society should provide the greatest rewards (income, prestige and power).

- Conflict theorists see a fundamental conflict between the powerful and powerless – or as Harold R. Kerbo put it, between the "haves" and the "have-nots". Discrimination and lack of opportunity prejudices the weakest in society.

- Symbolic interaction does not question why stratification exists, but looks instead at the impact it has on people's lives. The theory holds that most people's everyday interactions are with people like themselves. If you consider who you live, work and associate with, you likely share similar income levels and educational backgrounds. Even the food you eat, the way you dress and the music you listen to are probably similar. These interactions determine your beliefs, lifestyle and self-perception.

There are problems with these arguments. For instance, teachers can be viewed as a vital part of a functioning society, yet they do not reap the same financial rewards or social prestige as company CEOs or famous musicians. The sociologist Ralf Dahrendorf observed that many workers have obtained higher wages and greater job stability during the twentieth century. Social systems of inequality have become more complex and less rigid.

These counterarguments show that the original theories failed to explain why social stratification *persists*, particularly the importance of **ideology**. Values and cultural beliefs justify social stratification. For instance, the emphasis on meritocracy and self-determination in some societies reinforces the idea that people *deserve* their position in life based on their own effort (or lack thereof). But, as Daniel Markovits said, this frames structural inequality and exclusion as an individual failure and ignores the reality that "meritocracy favours the rich even when everybody plays by the rules". The complex structure of societies means that social standing has always been influenced by multiple factors and not merit alone.

Social class

Within sociology, the definition of class has been extensively debated. In Marxist terms, class is defined objectively in terms of one's relationship to the means of production. This was appropriate when people could easily be categorized as owners or workers, but the definition became unsustainable as working practices changed and social and cultural capital became more significant. In 1949, William Lloyd Warner identified three classes within American society: **upper**, **middle** and **lower** (with divisions of upper and lower within each). These distinctions were not defined by political status or power within communities and included non-economic criteria such as the ability to "act right" and social networks (explored later by Bourdieu – see p.55). Later sociologists proposed alternative ideas such as a "metropolitan class structure", the five-class model, the "semi-poor" and the "underclass". The common thread across all the theories is that social class has a direct impact on people's life chances. The rest of this chapter introduces you to some of these consequences and invites you to consider the factors that shape your own social identity.

Cultural capital

The French sociologist Pierre Bourdieu researched social class and argued that **meritocracy** (the idea that people get ahead based on their own accomplishments) is a myth that undermines people's chances of upward social mobility. He observed that natural talent and hard work are not enough to propel individuals up the social hierarchy due to the inbuilt bias against working-class people.

Building upon Marx's analysis of capital from an economic perspective, he argued that capital also exists in cultural, social and symbolic forms. Money is not the only source of power; knowledge, behaviour and cultural experiences – what he termed **"cultural capital"** – also contribute to an individual's success. One of the elements of cultural capital he identified was **"disposition"**, meaning the ways of thinking, perceiving and acting that we acquire and adapt according to the social world we live in.

SOCIOLOGY IS A MARTIAL ART

Bourdieu said that "sociology is a martial art" and "a means of self-defence" because it helps to reveal forms of domination and social inequality.

Habitus

Bourdieu also coined the concept of **"habitus"** to describe the set of **socially internalized dispositions**, or the socially accepted ways of thinking, acting and feeling, that influence the lives of individuals in each class. Your social interactions condition you to certain behaviours and acting them out creates and reproduces the habitus. Reading this book to yourself is an example of habitus – for centuries, across Europe reading was a social activity that took place in workshops and taverns, but by the nineteenth century "silent reading" had become common among the literate. Twenty-first century sociologists like Chin Ee Loh and Baoqi Sun analyzed how family habits around reading transformed it into a type of cultural capital.

Bourdieu observed that those of the same class share similar cultural values; how they presented themselves (such as their posture and clothing), their level of knowledge, way of speaking and choice of leisure activities were alike. Essentially, he argued that your class determines your tastes because you share the same habitus as your fellow class members, which in turn provides you with a sense of place or belonging. This habitus is essentially formed through socialization.

Socialization

Socialization is when individuals absorb the ideas, values and practices of their society. Socialization occurs at both a conscious and unconscious level throughout your life and in multiple forms, including:

- **Anticipatory socialization** – you learn the values and norms of a group you are expected to join, including a class, race or gender.

- **Class socialization** – you absorb the norms, values and behaviours expected of your social class.

- **Gender socialization** – you emulate the characteristics associated with your gender. This often occurs from birth with the choice of name and clothing (e.g. blue or pink).

- **Primary socialization** – your family exert influence over you. As Bourdieu explained, this is where you accumulate your cultural capital.

- **Secondary socialization** – behaviour learned from outside your family, such as your school or your peers. It can occur as an adult if you change careers or move countries.

Family

According to psychotherapist Esther Perel, "When you pick a partner, you pick a story, and then you find yourself in a play you never auditioned for." From the standpoint of sociology, the choice of stories you can choose from is endless, always evolving and remains significant because family is the most basic social unit upon which society is built.

The definitions of marriage and family have been hotly debated; put simply, marriage is a socially recognized union of two people and family is a socially recognized group that is usually connected by blood, marriage, cohabitation or adoption. Studies of marriage have been intertwined with family because the former has traditionally formed the foundation for the latter, though explanations differ according to the approach you take.

Functionalists view family as an "institution" that is vital for the stability of society; Talcott Parsons highlighted the purpose of "nuclear families" (two parents + children) in socializing children. The members of a family can also benefit from the physical and emotional support that relatives can provide.

Symbolic interactionists focus on the exchanges and shared understandings of family members. In 1945, Ernest W. Burgess and Harvey J. Locke observed that interpersonal relationships had become the basis of the family for the first time in human history (previously, the nature of the family was governed by external, primarily structural forces). This remains the case in the twenty-first century; in a 2010 study in the US, 60 per cent of respondents believed that if you consider yourself a family, you are a family. The more diverse and less structured forms of family have been explored by many sociologists.

FAMILY BONDS

Sociologists use the term **"family of orientation"** to describe the family you're born into, and **"family of procreation"** refers to one created through marriage. **"Kinship"** is used for immediate and extended bonds based on common ancestry, marriage or adoption (including cousins, uncles, etc.). Close friends that are treated like members of your family are **"fictive kin"**.

Family and conflict

Families can be seen to serve numerous social functions: they socialize children, deliver practical and emotional support, regulate sexual activity (according to the norms of a given society) and provide members with social identities such as class or religion. Conflict theorists also see some potential drawbacks. Instead of providing unlimited support and love, families can be the source of difficulties including stress, neglect, cruelty or violence. Families can also reinforce wider social inequalities, such as gender inequality or the transfer of wealth across generations.

AN "IDEAL HUSBAND"

Studies have found that social class can influence communication and expectations between spouses. In 1976, Lillian B. Rubin asked wives what makes an "ideal husband". Women in working-class marriages said those who don't drink too much and who go to work every day, while middle-class wives said those who communicate well and share their feelings.

Marriage

While marriage has been written about for thousands of years, mid-twentieth-century sociology paid closer attention to the phenomenon. As more data became available, attitudes towards divorce shifted, and family arrangements became "diverse, fluid and unresolved" (as Judith Stacey described it), and as a result, the scope for study became endless.

In countries such as the USA, dating patterns were being explored from lots of angles (such as class) and the results showed that interracial marriages increased (from 3 per cent in 1967 to 17 per cent in 2015) as well as the age at which people first married (in 1998 the median age was 25 for women and 26.7 for men, by 2021, the median age was 28.6 for women and 30.4 for men). These trends are now being replicated across the world. The USA has drawn a lot of attention in this area due to the culture's emphasis on individualism and liberty. The sociologist Andrew J. Cherlin has explored the conflict that this raises; the institution of marriage is still valued within society but so is the belief that "individuals who are unhappy with their marriages should be allowed to end them".

Families reinvented

Since 1990, marriage rates have declined globally, while instances of couples living together (known as **cohabitation**) have been increasing. The traditional family structure (a heterosexual married couple with children) is no longer the norm. These changes have brought new challenges. Ulrich Beck and Elisabeth Beck-Gernsheim identified a "status struggle" within relationships, reflecting "contradictions between family demands and personal freedoms". Increased gender equality and diminished family networks have boosted choice but also the risk of conflict (and divorce). As they put it, "When love finally wins it has to face all kinds of defeat."

FORMS OF COUPLING

Endogamy means marriage between people of the same social category, while **exogamy** is marriage between people of different social categories (e.g. working class and middle class). Sociologists also study **serial monogamy** (moving from one intimate relationship to another) and the idea of **"gradual exclusivity"** (slow dating) overtaking traditional courtship practices.

Love and intimacy

What is love? While sociologists don't have a definitive answer, they have explored the topic from various angles, such as friendship, parental love and the love of places. By interrogating different interpretations of romantic love, sociologists have discovered other trends in society. For instance, a 2013 study conducted in the UK by Julia Carter found women talked of "drifting" into and out of relationships in a way that suggested a lack of agency rather than freedom, and ideas of "the one" (i.e. the perfect romantic partner) prevailed due to this being normalized in social policy, media and commercial products.

TAMING AND CONSTRUCTING DESIRES

In the late twentieth century, Jeffrey Weeks noted that the institution of marriage was viewed as "healthy" and a way to regulate men's "natural" lustfulness. In this way, he said, "Social processes construct subjectivities not just as categories but at the level of individual desires." Other sociologists and philosophers viewed sexual desire as another social construction.

Gender

For decades, the discipline of sociology mirrored the gender inequality of society; most sociologists were men, research methods were from a male perspective and studies had largely focused on men. The domestic sphere was overlooked, despite its significance to society, and the division of private and public labour was not deemed worthy of investigation. The role of gender in society was ignored until 1949 when Simone de Beauvoir declared, in her book *The Second Sex* (1949), that "one is not born a woman: one becomes one". While there are biological differences between the sexes, she observed that women only become women because of their social circumstances (the norms that exist in their society).

SEX AND GENDER

The word "gender" used to be applied to masculine and feminine words in languages. In 1968, psychologist Robert J. Stoller made a conceptual breakthrough; he used the term **"sex"** to refer to his patient's biological traits and **"gender"** to the amount of femininity and masculinity a patient exhibited (as cultural categories). He thereby

In 1972, the term "gender" was brought into academic
and everyday use by sociologist Ann Oakley. In her book,
Sex, Gender and Society she wrote that "'sex' refers to the
biological division into male and female; 'gender' to the
parallel and socially unequal division into femininity and
masculinity". The two terms are not interchangeable.
Oakley argued that **gender is socially constructed** and
that gender roles create individual and gender identities.
This includes the norms, roles and behaviours usually
associated with being a woman, man, girl or boy, as well
as the relationships between these people. The division
of genders can be understood as socially imposed when
we recognize that characteristics of sex (the biological and
physical distinctions) remain largely the same globally
and historically, whereas gender varies across different
cultures and time periods. In the twenty-first century, as
more experiences of non-conformity are being reported
and studied, the challenge to dominant gender (and
increasingly, sex) norms means that the topic of gender
continues to grow in line with societal changes.

Gender socialization

From the moment you were born, your caregivers likely began to socialize you as either a boy or a girl (whether consciously or unconsciously). From the name you were given, to the games you played and your clothes, even your social interactions; these all contributed to your gender identity. In any children's clothing store today you will see a girl's section containing flowers and unicorns, and a boy's section dominated by dinosaurs and action heroes. Sylvia Walby called this social conditioning "training in one or the other set of gender attributes". With awareness, you can recognize this gender reinforcement in every aspect of life.

GENDER IDENTITIES

Not all cultures view gender as binary. A third gender is recognized in India and the Pacific Islands of Samoa, and in the West there is now more acceptance of various gender identities, such as genderfluid, bigender, agender and genderflux. Still, only a few countries permit an X gender marker on passports or allow people to change their gender marker on legal documents.

Agents such as family, education, peer groups and mass media maintain normative expectations for gender-specific behaviour, thereby reinforcing gender roles. People are also exposed to gender norms through secondary agents, such as the workplace or religion. Repeated exposure leads people to believe they are acting "naturally" based on their gender, rather than following a socially constructed role. Sociologists hold that the real-world impact of gender socialization cannot be overstated; it influences your appearance, behaviour, occupation, choice of partner and your self-esteem.

TERMS WORTH KNOWING

Gender expression is how a person presents gender outwardly, through behaviour, clothing or other perceived characteristics.

Gender identity is a person's internal sense of gender, whether man, woman, neither or both.

Transgender (or trans) refers to people whose gender identity or expression does not conform to their birth-assigned sex.

Non-binary is used by people who do not describe themselves or their genders as fitting into the categories of man or woman.

Trucks for boys, dolls for girls

The term **"gender role"** means the way men and women are expected to act and behave in any given society. They are based on norms, or standards, created by society. Sociologists have researched the gender norms reinforced by agents such as the following:

Family: Parents socialize sons and daughters differently, such as through childhood activities, expressions of affection and clothing. Sons may be spared domestic duties and asked to perform tasks that require physical strength, while girls are expected to be nurturing and neat.

Education: Male students receive more praise from teachers and greater leniency for breaking rules, while more obedience is expected from girls. School textbooks and literature reflect gender stereotypes and convey the subtle message that boys are more important and intelligent than girls.

Peer groups: Competitive sports are often encouraged for boys while girls play games that require cooperation and trust. Same-gender peer preferences (boys playing with boys, girls playing with girls) strengthen over time and promote biases about the other sex. This separation and lack of understanding continues into adulthood.

Mass media: The main characters in television shows and films (for children and adults) are often male, while females are frivolous or reinforce the idea that physical appearance is their most important feature. Magazines and advertisements trumpet the importance of beauty for females, and sports, cars and career success for males.

A FORM OF OPPRESSION

In 1974, Ann Oakley said the idea that domestic chores come "naturally" to women was rooted in cultural and historical processes. She found that housewives reported feelings of alienation more frequently than factory workers due to their isolation, lack of control or creative outlets. She argued that women were unable to reach their full potential because "housework is directly opposed to self-actualization". For the first time, being a stay-at-home mother started to be viewed as a form of oppression. Christine Delphy observed that the large amounts of unpaid work done by women would be paid for if it was done outside the family; hence "the marriage contract is a work contract".

Gender stereotypes

Expectations surrounding gender roles are based on oversimplified ideas about the attitudes, traits and behaviour patterns of males and females rather than inherent differences. Such stereotypes form the foundation of **sexism**, the prejudiced beliefs that value one sex over another. A 2001 study by Erin Leahey and Guang Guo showed few differences in mathematical abilities between boys and girls despite the male dominance in maths-related careers. Sociologists acknowledge the tangible effects of sexism, such as the gender pay gap and the higher proportion of men in high-earning jobs. The consequences of non-conformity are also explored, such as for men who take on feminine characteristics or the discrimination faced by transgender people.

CLASS AND GENDER EXPECTATIONS

In 2018, Katherine Fallon and Casey Stockstill found that single "elite women" (highly educated and high earners) in their thirties are commonly perceived as "unfinished adults", and that personal and professional success is overshadowed by the social "push to partner".

Gender performance

*Gender is a kind of imitation for
which there is no original.*
Judith Butler

The sociologist Judith Butler argues that if gender is socially constructed, then there can be multiple interpretations of it (that are often influenced by other social factors like class or race). She suggests that you have effectively been rehearsing gender throughout your socialization process, which leads you to then "perform" a gender identity in the way you choose to dress and communicate. Gender, then, is not who you are but what you *do*, and is only realized through its performance. If we behave in a way that is deemed socially "appropriate" for our sex, such as our mannerisms or choice of partner, we are imitating gender norms that are based on the ways that each sex behaves, and these "gender acts" determine our self-perception. In this way, she argues that different sexual identities (such as heterosexual, homosexual, transgender) all have equal validity because all sexual norms are also artificial.

The patriarchal ideal

In the 1980s, the Australian sociologist R. W. Connell coined the term **"hegemonic masculinity"** to describe a culturally idealized version of "manliness" within a hierarchy of masculinities. Common features, both globally and historically, include physical strength, competitiveness, assertiveness, independence, emotional reservation and heterosexuality. All men position themselves in relation to the dominant form of masculinity, and the pressure to conform then contributes to its reproduction. Men who embody the ideal are socially rewarded with greater status and power, while those that deviate from this standard can experience social isolation and humiliation (such as LGBTQ+ people). Women contribute to reinforcing the hierarchy through maintaining gender expectations of bearing children, as well as through their commitment to patriarchal religions and romantic narratives. Gender analysts have since used such insights to examine social attitudes and practices that perpetuate gender inequality, involving both men's domination over women and the power of some men over other (often minority groups of) men, and the effects on male mental health, violence, crime and society overall.

Sexuality

The topic of sexuality is closely related to sex and gender and refers to everything related to sexual behaviour, including attraction, arousal and desire. One aspect of sexuality that has been explored by sociologists from a variety of perspectives is **sexual orientation**. This refers to a person's physical, mental, emotional and sexual attraction to a particular sex (male or female) and is usually divided into the categories listed below although sociologists have expanded on these concepts to suggest that sexuality is a continuum rather than a strict separation.

- **Heterosexuality** is the attraction to individuals of the other sex (informally, "straight").

- **Homosexuality** is the attraction to individuals of the same sex (informally, "gay").

- **Bisexuality** is the attraction to individuals of either sex.

- **Asexuality** is no attraction to either sex.

- **Pansexuality** is attraction to people, regardless of their gender expression, gender identity or biological sex.

Constructing sexuality

Sociologists that adopt the symbolic interaction approach to society have argued that sexuality, like gender, is socially constructed. For instance, researchers have looked at **heterosexism**, which is the prejudiced belief that heterosexuality is the "natural" and "normal" expression of sexuality. Heterosexuality is standardized within social life and is founded in the dominant cultural belief across the world that there are two opposing sexes. In 1991, Michael Warner called this normalization of heterosexuality **"heteronormativity"**. Examples include the prevalence of heterosexual couples in mainstream media or insisting on the use of pronouns based on a person's biological sex rather than their preference (e.g. saying "he" rather than "they").

Those adopting the structural-functionalist perspective look at the ways that sexual regulation allows society to function and ensures the preservation of the family unit. Public policies and religious instruction that control sexual behaviour ensure marital cohesion, impact the number of babies born and dictate the forms of family that are permitted.

For instance, Jeffrey Weeks studied how laws in nineteenth century England reinterpreted and broadened the legal definition of homosexual acts, which encouraged the belief that heterosexuality was the only legitimate form of sexual behaviour. He viewed the promotion of marriage and heterosexuality as ideologically determined, and stated that "sexuality is as much about beliefs and ideologies as about the physical body".

Conflict theorists argue that the way sexuality is organized within society, such as through heteronormativity, creates and sustains social inequalities. It is essentially an expression of one dominant group maintaining power over subordinate groups (often women or non-heterosexual people).

BROMANCES AND WOMANCES

Eve Kosofsky Sedgwick used the term **"homosociality"** to describe non-sexual relationships between people of the same sex, such as friendship or mentorship. It is now used to refer to predominantly male occupations like sailing or same-sex arrangements, such as prisons or monasteries. In the twenty-first century, the term "bromance" entered popular culture to refer to a close homosocial relationship between two men, or "womance" between two women.

Education

A social institution that has attracted a lot of research is education. Sociologists have looked at **formal education** (structured methods of learning, such as a curriculum) as well as **informal education** (learning unconsciously or outside the classroom).

Informal education includes what Philip W. Jackson called the "**hidden curriculum**"; the unwritten rules and values of schools which reflect the wider society. Sociologists have explored the ways that schools prepare students for experiences they will encounter later in life, particularly in the workplace, such as workplace hierarchies, competition, rules and authoritative figures.

Functionalists view education as a necessary component of a functioning society. It can be seen to fulfil several purposes, such as socialization, social integration and engendering social innovation. For instance, Linda Schneider and Arnold Silverman found that schools in Japan teach children to value harmony and group belonging. Conflict theorists focus on how education promotes inequality, such as through standardized tests, and symbolic interactionists consider dynamics between students and teachers.

Education and inequality

Sociologists have explored the ways that social placing and standardized tests can perpetuate social inequality. For instance, studies have shown that teachers are influenced by the race and social class of students when placing students in groups according to "ability". The book *Schooling in Capitalist America* (1976) by Samuel Bowles and Herbert Gintis argued that education performs a vital role for capitalism: it ensures that working-class children remain working class and prepares young people for the "alienation" they will experience in their working life. Feminists have criticized the role formal and informal education plays in the socialization of children into traditional gender roles.

THE DIGITAL DIVIDE

The COVID-19 pandemic caused schools around the world to adopt distance learning practices and "home-schooling". Sociologists are researching the impact of this forced and sudden digitalization of learning and the inequalities between both schools and students in computer access and digital literacy.

Classroom dynamics

Symbolic interactionist studies of education look at social interaction across the school setting, including the classroom and playground. These studies help to explain structures and dynamics within wider society, which are rooted in the formal and informal lessons children learn at school. For example, sociologists have found a clear link between students' gender and their subject choices, as well as teacher expectations towards them.

The amount that a student learns is influenced by how a teacher labels them; children perceived as intelligent receive more attention and praise which causes them to learn more, and the reverse is true for children labelled as low achievers. The term **"self-fulfilling prophecy"** was coined by sociologist Robert K. Merton to describe this process which creates "a false definition of the situation evoking a new behaviour which makes the originally false conception come true". So, a child's reality eventually conforms to the teacher's original belief. Sociologists have also explored labelling through symbols of achievement. The concept of **"credentialism"** refers to the emphasis on certificates or degrees to show an individual's education.

The "popular" group

The **"hidden curriculum"** refers to non-academic knowledge gained in school, such as punctuality and obedience to authority, as well as the significance of **peer groups** (groups of people sharing the same social position, institution and commonly, age). James S. Coleman's research in the 1950s identified four types of peer groups: "nerds", "jocks", "leading crowd" and "burnouts". He found that your group affects how well you perform at school because you absorb the values and priorities of the group and what it associates "popularity" with, such as achieving high grades or sporting success. Group membership influences the personality traits you develop into adulthood.

THE ABCs OF FRIENDSHIP

Sociologists have found that "interpersonal attraction" (which leads to liking, friendship or love) is determined by proximity, or what is known as **"propinquity"**. In a 1974 study, Mady W. Segal found that police officers usually became friends with colleagues who shared the same first letter in their surnames because they were seated in alphabetical order.

Race and ethnicity

The study of race and ethnicity has been a central focus since the establishment of sociology as a discipline. Max Weber was one of the first sociologists to make a distinction between race and ethnicity. In 1906, he wrote that ethnic groups are not distinguished by "an objective blood relationship", but instead by a *belief* in shared descent and common customs. This notion of ethnicity being subjective later became a key feature of sociological approaches.

DISTINCT MEANINGS

Race is a social marker of a person's identity, typically based on skin colour and other physical or biological attributes that a particular society considers significant.

Ethnicity is associated with learned aspects of identity, such as language, culture, nationality or religion.

Minority group is a "subordinate group" within society, or one that lacks power. It is not necessarily a numerical minority as it can be used for any group that is disadvantaged by a dominant group (e.g. women or the elderly, even if they compose a large proportion of society).

Weber's view of race was not so unique, as he shared the popular opinion of the time that race stemmed from common biological traits. This view, known as **"essentialism"**, presumes that members of a race share unchangeable, inherited characteristics that have a biological component.

Essentialism was later challenged by W. E. B. Du Bois. He argued that racial identification is as subjective a process as ethnic classification, with the difference lying in the signs and boundaries associated with each. Thus, any perceived biological similarities a society attaches to a particular group, which it then labels a race, is just as subjective and open to change as the cultures or nationalities that are grouped together as an ethnicity. This view is shared by most sociologists today. An example of the subjectivity of race is the way that the "white" race category in the US census was redefined over the last century and continues to be debated today. As the journalist Arwa Mahdawi commented, "What really defines whiteness is not melanin or nationality – it's power."

Racism

Racial categories are understood by sociologists as a social construction, much like gender and class. Although they lack any objective reality, race categories have always entailed real consequences. Grouping people into different races means that people are treated differently, and often, unequally. Sociologists research racial tensions and inequalities using these concepts:

- **Prejudice** (racial and ethnic): preconceived attitude, beliefs and thoughts someone holds towards a group (**without reason or actual experience**)

- **Racism**: a form of prejudice that believes one racial category is superior to another. Individual racism refers to individual assumptions, beliefs and behaviours. Interpersonal racism is expressions of racism between individuals

- **Discrimination** (based on race or ethnicity): unjust or prejudicial behaviour towards a particular group

- **Colourism**: a form of prejudice based on skin tone

- **Systemic racism**: how society operates at large; this incorporates institutional racism and structural racism

- **Scapegoat theory**: first developed in 1939 by the psychologist John Dollard. This suggests that prejudice and aggression arise from frustration; the dominant group within society will shift blame onto a subordinate group for its problems, often a racial or religious minority.

- **Religious discrimination**: unjust or prejudicial behaviour based on a person or group's religious beliefs

- **Stereotypes:** simplified, mistaken generalizations about people because of their race and/or ethnicity

- **Multiple identities**: racial intermarriage including racial exogamy

Sociologists have attempted to explain racial and ethnic prejudices both between and within groups. One of the most popular arguments is **racial socialization**. This suggests that individuals who hold prejudiced beliefs have simply conformed to those of their social circle. Alternatively, the **group threat theory** proposes that economic and political competition increases racism. For instance, Susan Olzak argued that prejudice increases when two or more ethnic groups compete for the same jobs or housing (**ethnic competition theory**).

Theories on race

The three main sociological paradigms have made arguments for why societies maintain racial and ethnic categories, and similarly, racial inequality. Functionalists like Manning Nash assert that racial prejudice allows the dominant group within society to morally justify its suppression of one or more subordinate racial groups.

Conflict theorists have instead focused on the role of power between dominant and minority groups. Robert Blauner developed the **internal colonialism** theory to suggest that there are domestic forms of colonialism within the US which are comparable to how European colonial powers treated people on the land they occupied. Furthermore, Edna Bonacich argued that the common foundation of prejudice is the conflict between an indigenous working class earning higher wages than immigrant labourers.

For symbolic interactionists, race and ethnicity provide individuals with a source of identity and status. Herbert Blumer posited a **"sense of group position"** that suggests interactions between members of the dominant group allow racist views to form.

Migration

A key area of race and ethnicity studies is migration, including the racism experienced by migrants. Sociologists have explored the complex factors that cause people to become permanent settlers or temporary workers, as well as forced migrants like refugees. Robin Cohen distinguished three types of migrant:

- **Citizens** – those with full citizenship rights such as voting rights.

- **Denizens** – those welcomed by the state, such as billionaires or highly skilled employees.

- **Helots** – those performing poorly paid work, including illegally trafficked workers and legal workers such as domestic servants.

Media depictions of migrants have been an ample source of research, with studies showing that news media frequently portray those seeking asylum as an economic and security risk. Majid KhosraviNik revealed how discourse of the "threatening refugee" occurs across the UK print media – regardless of the political stance of the newspaper.

A global society

Globalization is the term used to describe the increasing and ongoing interconnectedness of nations across the world, and the breaking down of barriers between societies. Although international trade networks had existed for centuries, advances in technology, travel and communication at the end of the twentieth century caused a colossal acceleration of the process. As David Held defined it in 1999, the "widening, deepening and speeding up" of globalization touched on all aspects of society, "from the cultural to the criminal, the financial to the spiritual". This increasing interconnectedness became a central focus of sociologists who debated its causes, consequences and various forms, including the following:

Economic globalization – this considers the increasing movement of goods and services between countries, and dependence on technology. For instance, David Harvey argued that the need to speed up global flows of capital drove scientific and technological advancements, causing a "time-space compression".

Cultural globalization – researchers have looked at the intermixing of cultures and increasing knowledge of different countries, beliefs and religions.

Political globalization – sociologists have looked at the growth of the worldwide political system and the increasing power of international political bodies like the United Nations.

In 1993, George Ritzer argued that institutions and organizations around the world were adopting the same principles as the fast-food chain McDonald's; prioritizing efficiency, predictability, calculability and control. He described this new social order as **McDonaldization**, and believed that its effects could be felt throughout society, impacting areas such as our values, identities and relationships.

THINK GLOBAL, ACT LOCAL

While sociologists acknowledge that certain cultural forms have become global, they also recognize that **heterogeneity** remains. For instance, global goods and services have been adapted to accommodate the specific needs of consumers in local contexts; a trend that Roland Robertson described in 1992 as **"glocalization"**. There is a homogeneous universal culture, but with heterogeneous aspects that change from place to place. Examples of businesses going "glocal" include Starbucks replacing coffee-based drinks with aromatic teas in China.

Nationalism and multiculturalism

In 1983, Benedict Anderson proposed the controversial concept of **"imagined community"**. He defined nations as imagined political communities given that the citizens of even the smallest nations will never meet all their compatriots, but "in the minds of each lives the image of their communion".

An idea that developed alongside this discussion of national identity was **"multiculturalism"**, meaning the coexistence of multiple cultures in one nation. Sociologically speaking, two primary theories are commonly used to explain this integration:

- **Melting pot theory** – assumes individual cultures are abandoned in favour of the dominant culture of the nation. The forced assimilation of Indigenous peoples into American society is an example of this.

- **Salad bowl theory** – assumes members of different cultures can coexist peacefully. Cities with many ethnic communities can be viewed as salad bowl societies.

Sociologists have long been exploring the struggles individuals face when it comes to their nationality, race, ethnicity or other identity markers (e.g. gender, religion, etc.). In 1996, Stuart Hall argued that cultural identity is not only a matter a "being" but of "becoming". He believed that, with increasing awareness of and identification with the traditions, values and beliefs of other societies, modern identity was characterized by constant transformation, "increasingly fragmented and fractured; never singular but multiply constructed" and transcending both time and space.

In the twenty-first century, sociologists have been considering the rise in the formation of political alliances by people who share a common identity (known as **"identity politics"**), and the consequences of this trend for wider society.

SLOWING DOWN?

Since the global financial crisis of 2007/8, sociologists have been debating whether global integration is slowing down. This trend was given the name **"slowbalization"** in 2015 by futurologist Adjiedj Bakas. Central to the discussion is whether the drive for efficiency is being replaced with security, reliability and resilience.

Deviance

Until this point in the book, you may have had the impression that society is largely made up of people conforming to dominant social values, norms and roles. The flip side to this is that every society also includes large swathes of people rebelling against those very standards and rules, for which societies have created social and legal consequences for many of these actions.

Deviance refers to behaviour that breaks the rules, norms or expectations of a society. It has been an area of huge interest for sociologists due to the questions it raises, from how a society defines unacceptable behaviour to the reasons why individuals commit such acts. Deviance is relative (according to the location and time in history) and is usually dependent on the context and reasons for the behaviour (such as killing in the context of war). Sociologists, particularly from the structural-functionalist perspective, also recognize that there can be benefits to deviant behaviour – such as actions that challenge unjust social norms but inspire political movements and social change.

Forms of social control

Sociologists have analyzed the many formal and informal ways in which societies try to encourage conformity to social or cultural norms. The term **"social control"** is used to describe this regulation and enforcement of norms. The reason for social control is generally to maintain social order, and the methods used to enforce the social norms are known as **sanctions**. Sociologists have explored positive sanctions used to celebrate conformity and negative sanctions which are used to punish or discourage nonconformity.

TERMS TO KNOW (COINED BY WILLIAM GRAHAM SUMNER)

Folkways, or informal norms, are norms based on everyday cultural customs. They usually relate to practical matters, such as how to stand in an elevator, what type of clothes are appropriate for different situations or how to greet someone politely.

Mores (pronounced more-rays) are more serious moral injunctions or taboos that are broadly adopted in a society, such as the incest taboo.

Sanctions

Sociologists classify sanctions as either positive or negative, and formal or informal. An example of a positive sanction is if you are awarded "employee of the month" for working hard, while a negative sanction would be losing your job due to being consistently late. Informal sanctions can occur during everyday social interactions. These are negative if you are seen to behave in an unacceptable or inconsiderate way, such as talking loudly in a cinema or jumping a queue. These types of actions may cause the people surrounding you to give you disapproving looks or comments. Alternatively, if you are polite and socially engaged, you might experience positive sanctions, such as a smile or expressions of thanks.

In other scenarios, you may experience more serious sanctions that are formally recognized in some way, such as a speeding ticket for driving too fast or arrest for committing a crime. Sanctions can also be imposed on a country to change its behaviour if it has violated international law, typically through trade restrictions.

Socialization and deviance

Talcott Parsons argued that conformity was not achieved solely through the threat of punishment by external authority figures, but also by individuals internalizing norms and values through socialization. David Matza's seminal work on juvenile delinquency in the 1960s supported this theory and proposed that those who break society's rules are not necessarily different from the rest of us. He emphasized the fact that most young people, most of the time, did not break the law, and that when they did it was usually not very serious. Most delinquency consisted of "episodic" acts rather than a long-term commitment to a delinquent culture and way of life. He proposed that the development of an identity as a deviant involved a level of "affiliation" with others who shared the deviant identity, and the influence of authorities, both in defining the behaviour as deviant in the first place and responding to the individual who engaged in it, which Matza called "**signification**".

Crime

Deviant behaviour that breaches the rules or laws of a governing authority is considered a crime. Unlike torts, which are offences against private persons (that can lead to civil action), crimes are viewed as offences against the public or the state. This means that the classification of crimes and responses to them are dependent on the culture and the political environment of each society. These variations also influence the allocation of resources, police budgets, statistical crime rates and public perceptions of safety. Individuals that commit crimes can also be viewed from different angles; you may have watched television shows that explore the psychology of renowned criminals or come across theories of criminality based on rational decision-making, and even body types. For instance, in the mid-twentieth century William Sheldon proposed that athletically fit individuals were more prone to committing violent acts.

Sociologists, on the other hand, question the impact of social environment and social interaction for the commission of crime. Their findings often pose remarkable solutions for how to reduce these behaviours.

SOCIAL ECOLOGY AND CRIME

Sociologists since the late eighteenth century have been analyzing the social and physical characteristics of urban neighbourhoods that have high rates of crimes. In the 1920s, Robert E. Park and Ernest W. Burgess developed a theory of **urban ecology** which proposed that cities are environments, just like those found in nature, and are governed by many of the same forces that affect natural ecosystems, such as competition. Studies have identified several characteristics that are commonly found in neighbourhoods with elevated crime figures, including single-parent households, high rates of poverty and dilapidated housing. These factors contribute to what Edwin H. Sutherland called **social disorganization**, or weakened social bonds, that undermine governmental controls and reinforce cultural traditions that support antisocial behaviour.

"BAD INFLUENCES"

Sociologists use the term **criminogenic** to describe a system, situation or place that is causing, or likely to cause, criminal behaviour. Common factors include substance abuse, criminal peers and dysfunctional family.

95

Theories of crime

Sociologists have looked at the causation of criminal activity, as well as possible ways to prevent it. Theories of crime can be grouped according to the three major paradigms: functionalist, conflict theory and symbolic interaction.

Functionalists argue that crime is both inevitable and necessary. For instance, Émile Durkheim proposed the following three functions:

- **Regulation**: it increases conformity as people are reminded of the consequences of breaching social norms.

- **Integration**: it boosts the social bonds of people reacting to the criminal behaviour.

- **Progress**: in situations where crimes reflect the beliefs and wishes of the wider population, or challenge people's views, it can lead to legal reforms and positive social change.

Others such as Herbert J. Gans have highlighted the huge number of jobs that crime prevention and management provides, such as police officers and prison guards.

The following **functionalist explanations** for crime have been influential in sociology:

STRAIN THEORY

In 1938, Robert K. Merton proposed that some individuals commit crimes because they are responding to a situation, such as unemployment or poverty, that prevents them from achieving the goals that society prioritizes, especially economic success.

DEVIANT SUBCULTURES

Albert K. Cohen and Marvin Wolfgang argued that poverty and other social conditions produce criminal subcultures. These subcultures attract people who then acquire values that promote deviance. In 1955, Cohen proposed that boys who are failing in school experience **status frustration** and low self-esteem, causing them to seek groups that reward deviance. Walter B. Miller's **focal concerns theory** (1962) claimed that the values of working-class boys make crime more likely, namely; excitement, toughness, smartness, trouble, autonomy and fate.

Social bonds

Travis Hirschi's **social control theory** (1969) suggested that crime results from weak **"bonds of attachment"** and feelings of disconnection. The "typical delinquent" is young, single and unemployed. Many studies have found that weak relationships with parents or school make deviance more likely.

Conflict theorists look at the factors that give rise to criminal behaviour. In 1916 Willem Bonger argued that capitalism encourages egotism and greed, so people living in capitalist societies are more likely to break the law for personal gain. Conflict theorists have highlighted the power that legislatures have in making criminal laws that will benefit them, while the rest of society suffers the consequences. Feminist perspectives also emphasize the impact of gender socialization and inequality regarding crimes committed against women, such as rape, sexual assault or domestic violence.

Though conflict theories have sparked a great deal of controversy over the years, many studies support the view that the roots of crimes committed by people experiencing poverty lie in social inequality and economic deprivation.

Symbolic interaction theories focus on how behaviours come to be viewed as deviant or conventional by society, and why some people are more likely than others to be labelled criminals (due to class, race or appearance). This approach sees crime as a social construct.because there are no inherently deviant acts. Edwin H. Sutherland's **differential association theory** proposed that criminal behaviour is learned from others who teach you how to commit crimes and convince you that it is acceptable. He found that friendship groups affect criminality, especially during adolescence.

MORAL ENTREPRENEURS

Howard S. Becker's **labelling theory** argued that an act itself cannot be deviant; it is determined by how the powerful respond to it. What is considered deviant changes over time and varies across cultures. For instance, laws around the world differ as to whether the possession of cannabis is a crime. He used the term **"moral entrepreneurs"** for the people in a society who have the power to create the rules and labels.

The meaning of work

Many early sociologists analyzed the growth of capitalism and the changing nature of people's working lives. Developments in the twentieth century inspired new areas of research for sociologists studying jobs and organizations. These areas included occupational mobility, growing inequalities between and within professional occupations, as well as non-standard work arrangements (such as temporary, contract and part-time work). The following issues also stimulated debate:

Outsourcing (or subcontracting): the motives and outcomes of contracting activities to outside sources, rather than internally within an organization. Often seen to increase efficiency and provide competitive advantage by harnessing the specialist skills and experience of the outsourced supplier.

Digitalization: the global trend of adopting digital technologies as well as concepts, such as Internet of Things (IoT), big data, mobile applications, augmented reality and social media.

Automation: the process of introducing technologies to automatically execute a task previously performed by a human or one that is impossible to perform by a human.

Dual-labour market theory: a division of the economy into a "primary labour market" with high-paying jobs and benefits, and a "secondary labour market" with low-paying jobs and little job security.

Workplace polarization: service sector workers and educated professionals are in high demand compared to people with mid-level skills and education.

Knowledge divide: a division between those who are able to access, create, utilize and disseminate knowledge and those who cannot.

Dual-career households (where both adult members of the household pursue careers and maintain a family at home) provide sociological research opportunities. Arlie R. Hochschild pioneered the term **"second shift"** in 1989 to describe the household and childcare duties that follow a day's work outside the home. She observed that working mothers assume most of the responsibility of the second shift – equivalent to one month of labour more than their spouses every year. Sociologists studied the lockdowns necessitated by the COVID-19 pandemic and observed that gendered inequality remains in times of crisis; women across the world assumed a disproportionate amount of the childcare and home-schooling duties.

The purpose of work

The answer to the question of why people work may seem obvious: to make money. But sociologists have discovered time and again that there is a deeper motivation than financial security. For instance, Max Weber highlighted the concept of a religious belief in work as a way towards salvation. A pioneering study by Nancy C. Morse and Robert S. Weiss in 1955 showed that work was a central life interest for most Americans: 80 per cent of men said that they would continue to work even if they did not have to do so for economic reasons. They were also the first to survey responses to the question: "If you won the lottery, would you continue to work?" They found that the answer was overwhelmingly "yes".

WORK CENTRALITY

"Work centrality" is the term economic sociologists use to describe the belief that work is important in a person's life. Numerous studies suggest that work centrality is transmitted within the family (from parents to children), and to a lesser extent, through cultural background and social institutions.

Consumer culture

A development that has fascinated sociologists is the transition from a type of capitalism that valued frugality and money-saving to a "consumer society" where material wealth became a defining feature of a person's social status. Some perceive this shift as an inherently bad thing. Jean Baudrillard argued that society is now organized around consumption and that individuals gain prestige, identity and standing through their displayed purchases. Zygmunt Bauman wrote in 2007, "Consumer society thrives as long as it manages to render the non-satisfaction of its members (and so, in its own terms, their unhappiness) perpetual." He observed that all social classes are attracted to consumerism and judge themselves based on their ability to consume, resulting in inequality between "successful" consumers, who can afford luxury items, and "failed" consumers, who are unable to do so.

Others have defended consumerism as being an expression of human intellect and emotion. For instance, in Helmuth Plessner's *The Limits of Community* (1924) he pointed to the human desire for imagination rather than the immediate and material.

Consumerism and fantasies

In 1987, Colin Campbell developed the theory that consumer culture is rooted in the ideals of nineteenth century Romanticism, which emphasized the pursuit of pleasure and novel experiences. He suggested these same desires are what motivate individuals to buy goods and services that are not a necessity but a luxury. More recently, Alan Bryman argued that the inclination to consume is increased through blurring the distinction between reality and fantasy (what he calls "**Disneyization**"). Daniel Miller has presented consumerism as a potential source of social cohesion, as being ultimately "about the intensity of relationships with the people you care most about or live with, about status and local symbolic systems".

Urban sociology

Antonio Gramsci famously wrote that "the challenge of modernity is to live without illusions and without becoming disillusioned". One of the major aspects of modernity was the urban environment that was born out of the industrial revolution and the growth of capitalism. In the early twentieth century, the sociologist Georg Simmel conducted pioneering studies of the interrelation of space and social interactions. He found that the transition from rural communities to modern cities created mechanized societies that encouraged individualism, and that interactions within cities became increasingly financial. In his 1903 essay *The Metropolis and Mental Life,* he claimed that "the modern mind has become more and more calculating". For the first time, physical space was no longer seen as a passive, empty container for society and history, but a powerful element of social life. By the 1960s, sociologists like Jane Jacobs and Henri Lefebvre argued that people living in cities should take control of their environments to allow for more social and community spaces.

What is a city?

While the study of cities is a prolific area of interest within sociology, there remains no globally recognized definition of the term "city" itself. There are also stark differences in the global experience of **urbanization**. The following expressions have often been used to distinguish between urban areas around the world:

- **Suburbs** – communities surrounding cities, usually close enough for a daily commute.

- **Exurbs** – communities that exist outside the ring of suburbs, often wealthy and more spacious areas.

- **Slum cities** – unplanned shantytowns or squats on the outskirts of cities with no access to clean water, sanitation or other services. There are estimated to be 200,000 slum cities globally.

- **Global cities** – centres for financial and corporate services, often providing a technical and information infrastructure and a pool of human resources. These cities are often detached (economically and socially) from their national locations. Examples include London, Tokyo and Paris.

SOCIOLOGY TODAY AND TOMORROW

Kai T. Erikson wrote in 1997 that "sociology often has the look of a field devoted to the study of the perfectly obvious". In the twenty-first century, the "obvious" issues that sociologists are grappling with are complex. They are not confined to any one discipline and are not centred within specific geographic boundaries. Sociologists are expanding their focus to tackle the **"wicked problems"** of today; climate change, global pandemics, poverty, economic crises, income disparity and so on – challenges that are difficult or appear impossible to solve because of their intricate and interconnected nature. As a result, sociologists are conducting more interdisciplinary work and adapting their research practices as more big data sets become available. This chapter will introduce you to some of these major current and emerging concerns, and demonstrate the invaluable role that sociology can play in offering perspectives and solutions that are both innovative and practical. As Erikson also observed, a sociologist can "look for (and find) pattern" even in the midst of disorder.

Environmental sociology

You may have noticed that most of this book has discussed theories regarding modern society's impact on individuals and groups (and vice versa). This is because over a century of sociological debate has centred around human affairs without considering environmental impact. The discipline was founded on the premise that society is socially constructed, not determined by nature. This started to change in the 1970s with the emergence of the **environmental movement**. Sociologists, such as Riley E. Dunlap and William R. Catton, Jr., pointed out that the reciprocal relationship between environment and society had been neglected by scholars in their field. They coined a new theoretical outlook for sociology: the **New Ecological Paradigm (NEP)**. The subfield of environmental sociology was established and has been expanding ever since.

In the twenty-first century, climate change is the most important topic of research among environmental sociologists. Aside from being a major environmental concern, climate change is also viewed as a significant global justice issue and one that will continue to be felt for decades to come, even if major steps are taken to mitigate its harms.

Climate change

A sociologist may not be the first person that comes to mind when you consider expertise on climate change. However, as the rest of this book has demonstrated, sociologists are concerned with every facet of society. Climate change issues are embedded within institutions, cultural beliefs, values, production and consumption. Sociology is a vital part of the effort to understand and address this problem, particularly concerning the following questions:

- 🧍 How does modern human society drive climate change?

- 🧍 What impact will climate change have on society?

- 🧍 How has society responded to the threat of climate change?

WHAT IS CLIMATE CHANGE?

Climate change refers to long-term shifts in temperatures and weather patterns. Shifts can be natural, but research shows that human activities since the nineteenth century have been the main driver of climate change, primarily due to burning fossil fuels like coal, oil and gas.

SOCIAL CAUSES OF CLIMATE CHANGE

Sociologists have conducted extensive research into the various social factors that contribute to climate change. They have generally found two principal driving forces: **population growth** and **consumption**. One argument, known as the **treadmill of production theory**, proposes that the capitalist system has prioritized economic growth over social equality and environmental protection. Another argument, known as the **ecological modernization theory**, suggests that the need to protect the environment from the strains of human development will naturally present itself as society continues to develop.

IPAT

The IPAT equation, sometimes written as I = PAT or I = P x A x T, expresses the idea that environmental impact (I) is caused by three factors: population/number of people in a society (P), affluence/consumption in a society (A) and technology/amount of pollution (T). It was first proposed by two scientists named Paul R. Ehrlich and John P. Holdren in the 1970s to calculate the impact of humans on the environment.

CONSUMPTION AND CLIMATE CHANGE

Sociologists are contributing to the political and economic analyses of climate change. Studies have linked carbon emissions to economic and social organization in modern industrial societies, including political organizations, resource extraction regimes and population demographics. Sociologists have also found that individuals' and household consumption patterns contribute to climate change. Consumer culture that is motivated by status or competition results in the purchase of big cars, large homes, frequent vacations and other carbon-intensive luxuries. Conversely, if "green products" become markers of high status (such as electric cars, renting fashion or solar roof installations), consumption patterns could reduce emissions.

THE ANTHROPOCENE

The Anthropocene Epoch is an unofficial unit of geologic time, used to describe the most recent period in Earth's history when human activity has been the primary influence on the planet's climate and ecosystems. Some suggest that it began with the industrial revolution, while others argue that it was triggered by the atomic bombs that were dropped in 1945 during World War Two.

SOCIAL CONSEQUENCES OF CLIMATE CHANGE

Sociologists bring their distinctive awareness and understanding of inequality to the study of global climate change. Research has consistently highlighted how climate change is fuelling inequalities within and between countries. The people who are the most vulnerable – notably Global South regions and Indigenous peoples – are the least accountable for the emissions that trigger climate change. Studies have also extended beyond differences in wealth to inequality between genders, adults and children, and present and future generations.

SOCIOLOGY OF LOSS

Rebecca Elliott has argued that sociology should engage with the problems of loss (such as depletion, disappearance and collapse) that climate change entails. Unlike the dominant approach of "sustainability", Elliott observes that "the sociology of loss examines what does, will, or must disappear rather than what can or should be sustained". Examples include the disappearance of land, "degrowth", "downshifting" and reduction in resource-intensive practices.

A MAJOR GLOBAL PROBLEM

Sociologists recognize that climate change is an important dimension of social transformation. The present and expected consequences of climate change include the following:

- 👤 Extreme events – floods, fires, heat waves and drought.

- 👤 Rapid declines in essential needs – food, energy and water. In the twenty-first century, this began to unfold anew in some places (e.g. the US southwest), and intensify in regions already defined by scarcity (e.g. east Africa).

- 👤 Social disruption – the loss of livelihoods, homes and entire communities, and subsequently large movements of people (which explains the need for a sociology of loss).

- 👤 Material impacts – the cost of disaster recovery, rapid devaluation of real estate and stranded assets associated with energy transition.

Every individual around the world is affected by the climate crisis differently; hence sociologists serve a critical role in explaining the intersecting vulnerabilities at stake.

An emerging impact being explored by sociologists is the link between climate change and working practices. Working conditions in regions or occupations that are highly vulnerable (e.g. outdoor work in extreme heat) and the effects of policies and changes to trade (e.g. degrowth and "just in case" supply chains) have multiple consequences for families, communities and societies. Sociologists are also expanding their research to include the many non-material consequences associated with the loss of home, occupation or community. Charlotte Jones and Roman Krznaric are exploring the challenge of intergenerational climate justice, arguing that we need to understand ourselves as both inheritors and testators of the future.

REDUCED WORK HOURS

Studies show that working hours are strongly associated with carbon emissions. Countries that have reduced average hours, such as those in Northern Europe, are lower emitters. Households with less free time engage in more carbon-intensive consumption. Sociologists are exploring whether reducing paid working time would result in the "double-dividends" of reducing emissions and improving well-being.

SOCIAL SOLUTIONS TO CLIMATE CHANGE

People find it hard to give the same level of
reality to the future as they do to the present.
Anthony Giddens

Sociologists have made it clear that responding to climate change has less to do with technology and economics, where attention is so often directed, and more to do with power and politics. Information is not sufficient to motivate climate action; to change people's habits, the complex socio-cultural factors that shape individual behaviour must be understood first. For instance, studies have looked at the strategies used to promote climate denialism among conservative media outlets, how distrust in science has become a source of social identity for some people, and how political, industry and media coalitions maintain their cultural power. Evidence shows how disinformation was used for decades by representatives and allies of the fossil fuel industry to postpone proactive policy responses, and how media institutions weakened the perceived risks of climate change.

FUTURE DISCOUNTING

In his 2009 book, *The Politics of Climate Change*, Anthony Giddens tried to explain the reluctance of governments around the world to address the causes of climate change. He argued that the threat of future dangers and catastrophes is not enough to stir people into action because these dangers are not immediately visible in everyday life.

Technological fixes are not enough to effectively respond to climate change; studies have shown why these efforts must occur alongside other influences on human behaviour, such as social, political and economic structures. Sociologists have therefore been approaching climate change mitigation from multiple angles, including the possibilities of different governance arrangements, and institutional barriers that inhibit the creation of an eco-friendly economy.

Sociologists are also calling for shifts within the discipline itself, including increased funding opportunities, interdisciplinary collaborations (e.g. with natural scientists and engineers), and adding spatial or economic components to research. Greater representation of climate sociology scholarship from researchers in the Global South is also required.

BELIEFS ABOUT CLIMATE CHANGE

Sociology reveals how emotions and belief systems shape individual and collective responses to climate change, including climate anxiety, and how simultaneous crises around the world (such as wars or economic instability) are competing for public attention. The dominant ideologies of society determine if climate change is viewed as a problem and whether solutions to it are necessary. Ronald Kramer has been studying how sociological and cultural factors prevent individuals from talking about or acting on climate change. Kari Marie Norgaard's research showed that non-response is at least partially a matter of "socially organized denial".

EMOTIONAL IDENTIFICATION

Sociologists are also looking at the role of emotions in climate change debates. Ginger Jacobson has argued that emotion is fundamental to how people comprehend and experience environmental change, threats and conflicts. Stewart Lockie suggested that the way to bring the future into the present is to invoke joy in ways that are consistent with the routines of everyday life (e.g. commuting by bicycle rather than a private vehicle).

Population growth

When agricultural societies developed around 12,000 years ago, the entire global population stood at around 4 million people. By 1850 it had reached 1 billion and continued to grow at a staggering rate between then and the early twenty-first century, reaching 8 billion in 2022. All major forecasts expect it to peak this century – to about 10.9 billion by 2100 (according to the UNDP). This rate of population growth has inevitable consequences across nation states, including placing pressure on food production, water and energy supplies, as well as infrastructure and systems to support children and the elderly. The depletion of natural resources and increased carbon emissions caused by further growth is also a serious cause for concern. The study of these issues and the questions they raise is an area of sociology known as **demography**, which includes three important elements: fertility, mortality and migration. The economic, social, environmental and biological causes and consequences of population change are also explored.

Fertility

With the world population expected to increase by 36 per cent in less than a century, sociological research into the causes of population growth is vital for the national and international planning that this requires (including food production, healthcare and increased emissions of greenhouse gases).

The size and composition of a population is mostly determined by the rate at which babies are born (known as the **crude birth rate**: the number of live births per 1,000 people per year). Another important measurement is the **total fertility rate**, which is the average number of children that women have in their childbearing years.

CORNUCOPIAN THEORY

The cornucopian theory rejects the idea that population growth projections are problematic. The term comes from the cornucopia, the "horn of plenty", of Greek mythology. Cornucopians (also referred to as "boomsters") believe that environmental problems caused by a growing global population will be solved by human ingenuity and technological innovation.

While the global population is growing, there has nevertheless been a long-term decline in birth rates worldwide. The problem with low fertility is that it reduces population size not at all ages but only among the young and creates a momentum for future population decline. For a country to naturally replace its population, its birth rate needs to be at least 2.1, but in the twenty-first century, more than half of the world's population live in regions with below-replacement fertility. Sociologists have been exploring the effects of declining birth rates, including the following:

- Economic consequences – put simply, people of working age are needed to pay for goods, services, healthcare and pensions.

- Shrinking labour forces – impacts the rate of economic growth.

- Populations shrinking – due to low fertility rates, such as in Italy and Japan, and outward migration, such as in Poland.

- Ageing populations – if the number of retired citizens drawing on public pensions exceeds the number of workers this also raises an economic challenge.

Mortality

The sociologist Peter L. Berger wrote that human societies are made up of people "banded together in the face of death". But rather than theorizing about what happens to us when we die, sociological questions relate to where, how, when and in what circumstances we die. The related issues of bereavement and end of life care are also examined.

Understanding the overall growth of a population means analyzing the fertility rate and the **mortality rate**, which measures the number of people who die (known as the **crude death rate**: the number of deaths per 1,000 people per year). Sociologists are exploring the challenges that declining death rates bring for health and social care systems as well as families, communities, services and governments.

BEANPOLES AND SANDWICHES

Increased life expectancy and lower birth rates mean the **beanpole family structure** is more common (children have grandparents but fewer aunts/uncles). Middle-aged adults have become part of a **sandwich generation**, supporting their elderly parents and children.

Migration

A key part of studying populations is the movement of people from one area of the world to another, which is known as **migration**. This can take the form of **immigration**, which refers to movement into an area (a **destination point**) to take up permanent residence, or **emigration**, which describes movement out of an area (an **origin point**) to another place of permanent residence. Sociologists research forced, voluntary and involuntary forms of migration, as well as their consequences. For instance, the migration of academics and graduates can cause what is known as "brain drain" in the origin point. One example noted by Sansom Milton and Sultan Barakat is Afghanistan, where decades of conflict have caused an estimated 20,000 experts and academics to emigrate.

MOBILITIES

John Urry has argued that the impact and consequences of globalization can be understood through studying the movement of goods, people and ideas; what he calls "**mobilities**". Likewise, obstacles to movement (**immobilities**) reveal social exclusion and inequality.

Health

Medical sociology applies sociological theories and research methods to human health issues, medical institutions and their relationship to society. Factors such as race, gender, social class, sexuality and geographic location all contribute to human health outcomes. Culture also plays a critical part in shaping how health and illnesses are defined.

Questions about how to best prevent, identify and treat current and potential illnesses are not confined solely to medicine. Sociology can help us to understand social perceptions around health and illnesses, how diseases develop and spread within societies and issues around the patient/doctor relationship and medicalization.

SOCIAL CONSTRUCTION OF HEALTH AND ILLNESS

In 2010, sociologists Peter Conrad and Kristin K. Barker analyzed the research of medical sociology over the previous 50 years. They categorized the social construction of health into three areas: the cultural meaning of illness, the social construction of the illness experience and the social construction of medical knowledge.

Pandemics

Sociologists have long been interested in pandemics (diseases that spread across large areas). This is because they often disrupt the present social order and throw existing problems and tensions into sharp relief. For example, the impact of the COVID-19 pandemic starting in 2020 went far beyond people's physical health, with short and long-term repercussions in all spheres of social life, from employment practices to travel.

As societies evolve to be more global, sociologists have also been exploring the causes and distribution of diseases as well as the differences in high-income versus low-income countries.

PANDEMIC PATTERNS

Sociologists such as Philip Strong and Robert Dingwall have identified a recurrent pattern in pandemics, starting with an immediate moment of panic, which generates three consecutive societal pandemics: fear, explanation then action. These are followed by gradual acceptance and adaptation, where it settles into the background of everyday life and people find ways to live with it.

Ageing

The sociological study of ageing looks at the social aspects of both individual ageing and an ageing society. In the twenty-first century, people across the world can expect to live into their sixties and beyond, and every country is experiencing growth in both the size and the proportion of older persons in the population. According to the World Health Organization (WHO), the number of persons aged 80 years or older is expected to triple to 426 million between 2020 and 2050. Sociologists are researching the many changes that will be required in society, including:

- Increased supply of skilled and qualified care workers.
- New technology and infrastructure in hospitals.
- Government policies to provide the necessary frameworks.
- Greater preventive healthcare.
- Flexibility for workers with care duties.
- Work from home facilities.

Attitudes and beliefs about the ageing process are also studied extensively. Sociologists have found that societal changes over the past century have affected attitudes towards the elderly in many countries. Age, much like gender, race or class, is a hierarchy in which some categories are more highly valued than others. Researchers believe industrialization and modernization have reduced the power, influence and prestige once held by the elderly. For instance, Gunhild Hagestad and Peter Uhlenberg have noted the widespread segregation between the old and the young at institutional, societal and cultural levels, "with only the family surviving as an age-integrated institution".

RESPECT YOUR ELDERS

Studies have shown that the idea of respecting parents, elders and ancestors, known as **filial piety**, is a key virtue in Asian societies including Chinese and Korean cultures, but expectations and practices have been declining in the twenty-first century. Care is increasingly being given in financial rather than personal ways.

Obesity

Obesity, defined as abnormal or excessive fat accumulation (according to the WHO), has increased sharply in recent decades. Sociologists such as Stanley Blue and Elizabeth Shove reject the common public policy that concentrates on individual lifestyle choices and instead focus their research on the social and historical trends that, in combination, "shape the social body literally and metaphorically". By identifying what it is about contemporary society that is causing the obesity crisis, sociologists can help to identify adequate responses.

BIOHABITUS

Research shows that certain biological consequences (at the molecular and cellular level) of social experiences can be transmitted intergenerationally. The concept of **biohabitus**, developed by Megan Warin while studying obesity, expands Pierre Bourdieu's notion of habitus to explain how the biological body is affecting and affected by social practices and history. For instance, food scarcity may give rise to a biohabitus geared to energy-saving.

The social causes of obesity are complex, with factors including lifestyle, education, occupation, cultural practices and living conditions all identified as playing a role in weight gain. High-calorie, energy-dense food options may be (or appear to be) more affordable, and limited work or transport options reduce people's physical activity levels. Environments experiencing deprivation, disorder or high crime have also been shown to be associated with higher odds of obesity. Several studies have found that car dependency has contributed to the rise in obesity, with sociologists exploring current and potential interventions to encourage people to reduce their car use (e.g. road pricing or cycle lanes).

A DOWNSIDE TO EDUCATION?

Around the world, we're becoming collectively more short-sighted (also known as myopic - so nearby objects appear clearly, but those further away look blurry). It is most prevalent in East Asian countries such as Singapore and Vietnam. Children are also becoming myopic at a younger age. Sociologists have been exploring how this trend can be reversed.

Technology

The technological innovations of the past century have transformed societies across the world. Developments in computerization, automation and communication have raised fascinating questions for sociologists to explore. For instance, how do media and technology impact society? Does access to information increase social engagement? Do new forms of entertainment distract us from pressing social issues? The internet and accessible international travel have also allowed social circles to expand in ways that were previously unimaginable – reshaping the very meaning of "society".

RESHAPING THE PHYSICAL WORLD

The sociologist Gerhard Lenski argued that technological progress is critical to the evolution and survival of societies. He observed that industrialized societies have more control over the impact of their surroundings (e.g. environmental fluctuations) and thus develop different cultural features. He believed that the more information (or knowledge) a society has, the more advanced it will become.

Technological stratification

Technology is the application of scientific knowledge to solve problems, and it is present in all aspects of society, from medicine to transport. However, the benefits and opportunities it provides are unequally distributed. Sociologists have been researching the ways that technological advancements increase social stratification:

- **The digital divide**: uneven access to technology by different races, classes and geographic areas (e.g. access to personal computer and internet use).

- **Knowledge gap**: the digital divide means people with less access to technology are deprived of knowledge or information (and its benefits).

CULTURAL BATTLE

Boaventura de Sousa Santos argued that the **Global North** have elevated science to a form of knowledge that is superior to all others. Global equality can only be achieved when non-scientific knowledge (that results in different cultures' practices) is acknowledged and respected.

Social media

Historically, shared geographic location was a key basis for understanding our relations to one another and our institutions. Today, sociologists are studying relationships formed through social networks, where geography no longer matters. Researchers seek to understand how technological development is affecting our interactions with one another and society more broadly. Amitai Etzioni suggested that communities – including those based on the internet – are social relations that are defined by shared norms and values rather than by proximity. He argued that the most effective sources of bonding and ideas about virtue come from communities, not from the state.

THE CYBER SELF

Charles Horton Cooley's concept of the looking-glass self (see p.34) has been explored in the context of virtual environments (e.g. avatars) and social media, where your reflection and others' judgements are no longer imagined but publicly shared. The cyberpsychologist Mary Aiken called the online version of social media users the "cyber self".

Constructed realities

The sociologist Jean Baudrillard wrote in 1981 that reality is that "which is already reproduced", meaning that representation had started to create reality rather than the other way around. He argued that "perfect" virtual worlds and cinematic portrayals of reality results in a rejection of real-life experiences. The screen depictions of reality (also called **hyperreality**) are far more attractive to us. He also observed that excessive information means that we are prone to accept the simple solutions handed to us. Today, **new media** (which refers to interactive forms of information exchange, including networking sites, blogs, podcasts and virtual worlds) decides what to prioritize, simplify and portray as reality – a process known as **gatekeeping**.

A ROBOTIC LIFE

Some sociologists have developed Karl Marx's idea that capitalism causes "alienation" from our human nature. Amitai Etzioni said that social systems that fail to protect basic human needs result in alienation. Erich Fromm believed that "synthetic smiles have replaced genuine laughter" and that we're all at risk of becoming robots.

Outrage and fake news

Ever since the anti-globalization protests in Seattle in 1999, sociologists have been analyzing the use of the internet to coordinate international political mobilization and coalition building. Social media provides alternative forums for those unable to access traditional political platforms, such as the Arab Spring protesters of 2011, who were able to spread information worldwide through social media. New opportunities have become available for creating, accessing and sharing information. However, there is no guarantee of the accuracy of the information offered. Rumours, **disinformation** (information that is fake or misleading) and **misinformation** (information which is fake or misleading and spreads unintentionally) have become challenges confronting media of all types. Even democracy is seen to be at risk; researchers have analyzed how misinformation influenced the 2016 USA Presidential election results. The immediacy of new media coupled with the lack of oversight raises questions about how we can ensure our news is coming from accurate sources. Sociologists are also exploring why social media use is linked to increased anxiety and depressive symptoms, negative body image, sleep problems and cyberbullying.

Human connection

Throughout history, technological revolutions have altered relationships and daily life. Sociologists explore how potential technological advancements in the twenty-first century have radically changed the way people interact and form connections. The study of **human-robot interaction** is growing alongside technological achievements in robotics. Elyakim Kislev believes further advances may give rise to "Relationships 5.0" whereby people develop feelings towards technology. While human-to-human relationships will continue, our emotional lives will undergo a gradual process of change due to the cognitive (AI), sensorial (virtual reality and augmented reality) and physical (robotics) revolutions that are expected to take place. For instance, "socially interactive robots" – that are designed to interact with human beings – are expected to become increasingly significant in everyday life. Simone Alesich and Michael Rigby have argued that gendering humanoid robots might transform human-to-human relationships and understanding of gender, and Sherry Turkle has questioned whether delegating our vulnerable moments to robots (such as caregiving to elderly or children) and communicating electronically will redefine what it means to be human.

Surveillance societies

The **panoptic surveillance** envisioned by Jeremy Bentham and later analyzed by Michel Foucault (see p.43) has been increasingly realized in the twenty-first century. Digital security cameras capture our movements, our cell phones can be tracked and police forces around the world use facial-recognition software. The sociologist David Lyon has explored the expansion of what he terms "surveillance society", including the collection of **big data** regarding our financial situations, health, consumer preferences and qualifications – all of which require constant collection and updating. He also points out that much of the surveillance occurs without our knowledge and threatens to restrict our civil liberties. The widespread use of CCTV (closed-circuit television) is one example of surveillance that occurs without our consent, and we have no control over who observes us or the future use of footage. Sociologists have also studied how apparently neutral surveillance systems often reflect the prejudices of the operators.

Companies that provide you with free online services, such as search engines and social media platforms, are also conducting mass surveillance of the internet.

By collecting and scrutinising your online behaviour (purchases, searches, likes), they produce data that can be used for commercial purposes. You might have noticed this if you search online for a product and then receive constant advertisements for products related to it. This process, termed **surveillance capitalism** by Shoshana Zuboff, is expanding to new data sources like smart home devices, drones, connected toys and wearables. Zuboff has questioned the "knowledge asymmetries" that this creates, as surveillance capitalists undermine our autonomy through their power to "tune, herd and condition our behaviour" towards their most profitable outcomes.

Artificial Intelligence

> *Technological development is creating new*
> *threats and opportunities for humanity, putting*
> *the lives of future generations on the line.*
> **William MacAskill**

The term Artificial Intelligence (AI) generally refers to software (computing infrastructure and programming code) that can learn and act on its own. For example, smart assistants detect the tone of voice and preferences of their user, and self-driving cars learn and identify routes and obstacles. What counts as AI differs across a wide range of contexts and defining it is seen as an interpretative, political process.

Sociologists have been exploring the societal impact of AI, particularly regarding inequalities and structural change. Sociological theories and methods are being used to investigate the creation, use and effects of AI sociotechnical systems in a range of areas from healthcare, politics and systemic racism to social movements, policing and art.

In 2018, Safiya Umoja Noble challenged the popular assumption that search engines, such as Google, offer an equal playing field for all forms of identities and ideas. Her research showed that search engines replicate the racism and sexism found in everyday life. Sociologists have built on this approach to understand how inequalities are embedded in AI systems. The companies that produce AI systems often claim that algorithms or platform users create racist, sexist outcomes, but sociological studies have revealed that human decision-making occurs at every step of the coding process. Sociologists are also studying the large-scale data systems that are being used to train the AI systems. For instance, Taylor M. Cruz wrote in 2020 that the fundamental conditions of social inequality are not being addressed when the focus is on data collection alone. Kelly Joyce and Susan Bell have argued that an uncritical use of human data in AI sociotechnical systems is likely to reproduce and potentially exacerbate pre-existing social inequalities. Sociological guidance can bring social and institutional contexts into focus and help to make AI systems that promote equality.

Conclusion

You are living in a time of unprecedented change. Over the last century, the world economy has expanded at a phenomenal rate, as have the rates of literacy, international travel, social networks, scientific advancements, energy use, carbon dioxide emissions and digital technologies. This book has shown you the crucial role that sociology has played in our understanding of this transformation, often through ambitious research projects and innovative theories. In the approaching decades, more than 8 billion people are set to witness further societal change in ways that we can barely imagine today. By harnessing your sociological imagination and turning a critical eye to the norms and expectations of your society, you will have the benefit of gaining a greater understanding of yourself, the people around you and the evolving social environment in which you live. As bell hooks said, "To be truly visionary we have to root our imagination in our concrete reality while simultaneously imagining possibilities beyond that reality."

Further Reading

Raewyn Connell, *Gender: In World Perspective, Fourth Edition (Short Introductions)* (2020)

Oded Galor, *The Journey of Humanity: The Origins of Wealth and Inequality* (2022)

Daniel Markovits, *The Meritocracy Trap: How America's Foundational Myth Feeds Inequality, Dismantles the Middle Class, and Devours the Elite* (2019)

Michael J. Sandel, *The Tyranny of Merit: What's Become of the Common Good?* (2021)

Jennifer D. Sciubba, *8 Billion and Counting: How Sex, Death and Migration Shape Our World* (2022)

Mary Ann Sieghart, *The Authority Gap: Why Women Are Still Taken Less Seriously Than Men, and What We Can Do About It* (2021)

David Swift, *The Identity Myth: Why We Need to Embrace Our Differences to Beat Inequality* (2022)

Steven W. Thrasher, *The Viral Underclass: The Human Toll When Inequality and Disease Collide* (2022)

THE LITTLE BOOK
OF ANTHROPOLOGY

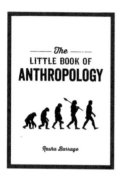

Rasha Barrage

Paperback

ISBN: 978-1-80007-415-6

This illuminating little book will introduce you to the key thinkers, themes and theories you need to know to understand the development of human beings, and how our history has informed the way we live today. A perfect gift for anyone taking their first steps into the world of anthropology, as well as for those who want to brush up their knowledge.

THE LITTLE BOOK
OF ECONOMICS

Shaun Rusk

Paperback
ISBN: 978-1-80007-719-5

If you think it's time you learnt how inflation works, what causes recessions and why the stock market is so unpredictable, then let *The Little Book of Economics* bring you up to speed on the basics of micro- and macroeconomics, and demystify the world of taxes, trade, investments and finance, in simple English and with easy-to-follow examples.

Have you enjoyed this book? If so, find us
on Facebook at **SUMMERSDALE PUBLISHERS**, on
Twitter at **@SUMMERSDALE** and on Instagram and
TikTok at **@SUMMERSDALEBOOKS** and get in touch.
We'd love to hear from you!

WWW.SUMMERSDALE.COM